Louis and Billie Van Dyke's

The Blue Willow Inn
COOKBOOK

Louis and Billie Van Dyke's

The Blue Willow Inn
COOKBOOK

Jane and Michael Stern

THOMAS NELSON
Since 1798

NASHVILLE   DALLAS   MEXICO CITY   RIO DE JANEIRO

Published in Nashville, Tennessee, by Thomas Nelson. Thomas Nelson is a trademark of Thomas Nelson, Inc.

Thomas Nelson, Inc. titles may be purchased in bulk for educational, business, fund-raising, or sales promotional use. For information, please e-mail SpecialMarkets@ThomasNelson.com.

ISBN 978-1-4016-0504-9 (TP)

Library of Congress Cataloging-in-Publication Data

Stern, Michael, 1946–
    Louis and Billie van Dyke's Blue Willow Inn cookbook / by Michael and Jane Stern.
        p. cm.
    ISBN 978-1-55853-991-4 (hardcover)
    1. Cookery, American—Southern style. 2. Blue Willow Inn. I. Stern, Jane. II. Title.
TX715.2.S68 S663 2002
641.5975—dc21   2002006035

Printed in the United States of America

13 14 15 16 17 QG 5 4 3 2 1

To my Mother,

our staff and our customers,

we dedicate this book and thank you

for your contribution to the success of

the Blue Willow Inn Restaurant.

—Louis Van Dyke

CONTENTS

FOREWORD

In 1985 we opened our first restaurant. The name was Billie's Classic Country Dining and it was located in a small cottage house in Social Circle, Georgia. Within eighteen months, the business outgrew the sixty-eight-seat restaurant. In 1987 we moved our business to nearby Covington to a larger location and changed the name to Billie's Family Restaurant. Several months later we took over the operation of a restaurant in Monroe housed in the American Legion Building. The restaurant had been ongoing since 1952. Due to significant structural problems (termites, leaking roof, etc), we closed our restaurant in Covington in 1989 and worked together in the Monroe restaurant. During that time the grand old southern mansion, now known as the Blue Willow Inn, became available.

We had both agreed, prior to opening our first restaurant, that we would follow Christian principles in the operation of our restaurant and in our relationship with our staff and customers. Before taking on such an overwhelming project as the Blue Willow Inn, we sought the Lord's will.

After receiving confirmation from the Lord, we signed the papers to purchase the old mansion the following day. Since opening in 1991, the challenges, experiences, and accolades have often overwhelmed us and at the same time humbled us. Back in the early days of our first restaurant, in 1985, I made a comment to Billie; "Wouldn't it be nice if one day we were considered to be the best at what we do?"

A dream? Considering the number of thousands of restaurant in the South cooking southern dishes, this could only be a dream.

We are living our dream. Our faith, hard work, loyal employees, and customers have all contributed to the success of the Blue Willow Inn Restaurant.

—Louis and Billie Van Dyke

INTRODUCTION

WELCOME TO THE Blue Willow Inn of Social Circle, Georgia. Social Circle is a small town a far piece from just about anywhere, nearly an hour into the countryside from Atlanta; and yet people flock from Atlanta to eat here; families come from Tennessee and the Carolinas for celebration meals, and travelers detour from I-95, 300 miles to the east, for lunch. To have a meal at the Blue Willow Inn, even if you're one of those lucky folks who lives close enough to visit once or twice every week, is an event. Every day—every meal— is a special occasion in this mansion that long ago inspired *Gone With the Wind* author Margaret Mitchell to conceive of Tara.

The Blue Willow Inn is a theme restaurant, the theme being Sunday Dinner at Your Southern Grandmother's House. Even if you never had a Southern grandmother, or if

you did have one and she was a lousy cook, you cannot help but feel the security of culinary tradition when you sink your teeth through the crust of a piece of succulent fried chicken or fork up a heap of spruce green collard greens sopped with pot likker and garnished with crumbs from a hunk of hot cornbread.

As at Grandma's house, you can eat your fill. At the heart of the Inn is the Walton Room. In this room is a grand buffet. After being served iced tea or lemonade at your table in one of the dining rooms of the mansion—say, The Savannah Room or The Garden Room—you pick up your Blue Willow plate and head for the Walton Room to select a meal: choose all of everything you want. You are welcome to return to the buffet with a new, clean plate for seconds, thirds, and fourths; but no matter how capacious your appetite, there is no way you will have a satisfying taste of the dozens of entrees, vegetables, and desserts set out for every meal.

The food is real Southern, which includes such time-honored classics as fried pork chops, buttermilk biscuits, and peach cobbler, as well as more modern expressions of the Dixie kitchen in the form of cheese-gooped, breadcrumb-enriched, butter-dripping casseroles. Every day the menu is a little different, but whenever you come to eat, you will find spread out before you on these magnificent buffet tables an edible catalogue of dishes that reflects the whole South. That includes the best of log-cabin soul food, country favorites from the tenant farmer's wood stove, the pride of the plantation kitchen, culinary fineries from old-fashioned ladies' lunch, and a passel of no-fuss formulas that reflect twentieth-century convenience cooking.

Don't be surprised that many of the dishes in this book use boxed and canned ingredients, and there are recipes galore that call for tubs of Cool Whip and packages of Jell-O. While proprietor Louis Van Dyke wouldn't dream of making mashed potatoes from a mix or cooking collard greens in any manner other than the slow, porky, old-fashioned way, neither would he make the glorious meal known as Chicken Divan without crumbled Ritz crackers or Savannah Shrimp and Rice without a can of Campbell's mushroom soup.

That's one of the many things we love about the Blue Willow Inn. Its menu is an expression of American food at its most exuberant, a crazy quilt of tradition and invention, time-honored ways and make-life-easy shortcuts. And that reflects the way most real grandmothers, in the South and elsewhere, really cook.

THE UPSHAW MANSION

The magnificent neoclassical home that is now the Blue Willow Inn was built by John and Bertha Upshaw because of sibling rivalry. In 1916 John's younger brother, Sanders, erected a magnificent house across the street from the modest cottage where John and Bertha lived. John decided not to be outdone by his brother. He and Bertha walked across the street with measuring tapes and surveyed every aspect of Sanders's place. Then they designed a near-mirror image, but bigger and better!

Completed in 1917, and no more than eighteen inches greater in most dimensions, the elder Upshaw home, now the Blue Willow Inn, outdid the original in many other respects. It is cream brick rather than wood; its roof is red tile rather than slate; where Sanders's house had double windows, John's has triples, which are anchored by granite sills. John built two porches where Sanders had only one; and when John laid oak floors, the boards were set, not side-by-side, but in a decorative pattern.

A view of the old Sanders Upshaw mansion through the door of the bigger Upshaw mansion.

Despite these differences and the changes and improvements made over the years, the reflective image of the two houses is stunning, for they are exactly aligned, front door to front door. When Social Circle's main street was still unpaved, a wooden sidewalk was built across it so that the families could visit one another without stepping in mud (yes, they remained close and friendly). Old-timers remember that when carriages drove past, the thump-thump of the horses' hooves suddenly became a clack-clack when they hit the planks that ran across the street. Today the grooves in the concrete sidewalks that lead from the street to the porches line up precisely. (The old Sanders Upshaw home remains a private residence.)

The Upshaw family bequeathed John and Bertha's property to the social clubs of Social Circle to be used as a community house, and through most of the 1950s the Bertha Upshaw Clubhouse was a social center for weddings, school dances, and town events. Civil rights battles of the late 1960s caused Social Circle's clubs to abandon the property, and by the time it was bought by the Reverend Homer Harvey in 1985 as home for his Church of God congregation, it was in dire need of repair and restoration. Rev. Homer Harvey's congregation renovated much of the exterior, but when they were ready to move to their own newly built church at the back of the property, the old home still needed plenty of work.

At that time Louis and Billie Van Dyke were operating a successful restaurant in the American Legion Hall in nearby Monroe, Georgia. They had fantasized about transforming the old Bertha Upshaw Clubhouse into a southern-themed

The Bertha Upshaw Clubhouse and Pool were abandoned and neglected from the late 1960s until 1985 when Reverend Harvey purchased it.

restaurant; but they knew they couldn't afford it. When Louis went to the bank for financing, he was shown the door. Such a grand place in such a small town simply did not make good business sense.

It was 1990. The asking price was two hundred thousand dollars in addition to all the money it would take to make necessary repairs and to create a commercial kitchen. After the bank said no, Mr. Harvey agreed to finance the whole deal for no money down. Louis and Billie took the plunge in the summer of 1990. They personally scraped paint, replaced wiring, and finished floors. For work they couldn't do, they bartered future meals. The Blue Willow Inn opened Thanksgiving 1991. Since that day it has served guests from fifty states and 150 countries; it has hosted royalty (when the Olympics were in Atlanta); and it annually wins *Southern Living* magazine's Reader's Choice award as Best Small-Town Restaurant in the South.

The Van Dyke's first restaurant, Billie's Classic Country Dining, opened in 1985.

DRINKS
and
BREADS

SWEET TEA

Iced tea is Dixie's eau de vie. It excites the palate, slips down the throat, and brings vigor back to bodies wrung out from the hot sun.

Throughout the Deep South, people drink sweet tea, which means that there is no need to add any sugar to what is served. It comes already sweetened. It is best drunk from a tall, wide-mouthed glass with clear, fresh ice cubes or heaps of crushed ice. Lots and lots of ice, always lots of ice. And, of course, a big pitcher for refills, as needed. If you wish, you can be fancy and squeeze a little lemon in it or add a sprig of mint, but really, any addition is gilding the lily. Sweet tea should be perfect just the way it is served—no garnish necessary. One important rule for making it is to use regular supermarket tea, not fancy gourmet tea. Another rule

is to make it sweeter than you think it should be. Indeed, the motto at the Blue Willow Inn is to serve tea "strong and just a little too sweet."

Many are the hot summer days when we have gulped multiple glasses of this tea, realizing that this and only this is the beverage that God meant parched southerners to drink. It quenches thirst, replenishes verve and vitality, and stimulates your appetite for a nice hot supper.

According to Louis Van Dyke, "Grandmothers and mothers of the Old South served sweetened iced tea at every meal. In the Old South, children were never allowed to drink iced tea until they were twelve years old. They drank milk, water, or lemonade. Soft drinks were never allowed at the dinner table. The Blue Willow Inn honors these traditions by serving only sweetened iced tea, lemonade, coffee, water, and—to the unfortunate—unsweetened iced tea. Soft drinks are not available.

---

1   *gallon water*
4   *to 5 family-size tea bags (each one is enough for a quart of tea)*
3   *cups sugar, at least*
    Lemon slices, for garnish (optional)
    Sprig of mint (optional)

Bring the water to a boil in a 1½-gallon saucepan. Turn off the heat, and add the tea bags. Cover and steep 12 to 15 minutes. For stronger tea, let it steep longer, up to 20 minutes. Add the sugar while the tea is hot, stirring vigorously until dissolved. Allow to cool; then pour over ice. Garnish as desired.

MAKES ABOUT 4 QUARTS

Veranda Tea Punch

Sweet tea and lemonade are the traditional beverages to drink before and during a Blue Willow meal; but for special summertime moments on the porch, this equally sugary punch is something completely different.

⅔	*cup sugar*
⅔	*cup water*
	Juice of 4 oranges
2	*cups strong-brewed tea*
1	*quart Coca-Cola*
1	*quart soda water*
	Lemon and orange slices, for garnish

In a large saucepan combine the sugar and water, and boil for 10 minutes to make sugar syrup. Cool. Mix the orange juice with the cooled sugar syrup. Add the hot tea. Allow to cool. Just before serving, add the Coca-Cola (or ginger ale, if preferred) and soda water. Garnish with lemon and orange slices.

MAKES ABOUT 3 QUARTS: 20 SERVINGS

Angel Biscuits

Leavened with yeast, these biscuits are airier and lighter than the traditional biscuit that comes with breakfast. They make a great choice for the breadbasket at suppertime.

1	package active dry yeast
2	teaspoons warm water (110°F)
4	cups flour
3	teaspoons baking powder
1	teaspoon salt
¼	cup sugar
½	cup solid vegetable shortening
2	cups buttermilk
1	teaspoon baking soda

Preheat the oven to 475°F. Sprinkle the yeast into the warm water in a small cup or bowl. Stir and give the yeast time to get frothy. Sift together the flour, baking powder, salt, and sugar. Cut in the shortening. Mix the yeast with the buttermilk, and combine with the flour/shortening mixture. Add the baking soda. Roll the dough out onto a lightly floured surface to about ¼-inch thickness. Cut with a biscuit cutter (a clean standard-size can works fine). Place each biscuit on a lightly buttered baking pan, and bake for 10 to 12 minutes until golden brown.

MAKES 15 TO 20 BISCUITS

Banana Nut Bread

This is more like dessert than it is bread to accompany a meal. For afternoon tea, or with morning coffee, it's just right.

½   *cup solid vegetable shortening*

1   *cup sugar*

2   *eggs*

1   *teaspoon lemon juice*

1   *cup mashed overripe bananas*

2   *cups all-purpose flour*

1   *tablespoon baking powder*

½   *teaspoon salt*

1   *cup chopped pecans*

Preheat the oven to 350°F. Grease a bread loaf pan. In a small bowl cream the shortening and sugar together. In a separate bowl beat the eggs until light and fluffy. Add the lemon juice and mashed bananas. Blend the eggs with the creamed shortening and sugar. Sift the flour, baking powder, and salt together, and mix quickly into the banana mixture. Add the nuts, if desired. Pour the mixture into the prepared loaf pan, and bake for 1-¼ hours, or until a toothpick inserted in the middle comes out clean.

MAKES 1 LOAF

Blueberry Muffins

Social Circle's Hard Labor Creek Blueberry Farm suggested this recipe to the cooks at the Blue Willow Inn. They're wonderful served warm from the oven, with softened butter to melt inside when you pull one apart.

1	egg
½	cup milk
¼	cup salad oil
1½	cups all-purpose flour
½	cup sugar
2	teaspoons baking powder
½	teaspoon salt
1	cup fresh blueberries, washed and dried, or
¾	cup drained, frozen blueberries

Preheat the oven to 400°F. Combine the egg, milk, oil, flour, sugar, baking powder, salt, and blueberries, mixing lightly. Do not overmix. Pour into a dozen lightly greased muffin cups. Bake for 20 to 25 minutes.

MAKES 12 MUFFINS

Buttermilk Biscuits

Having grown up in Savannah, the Van Dykes know just how important biscuits are as part of a big southern-style restaurant meal. They dined often at Mrs. Wilkes Boarding House on Jones Street, famous for its bountiful all-you-can eat meals. They always include plenty of buttermilk biscuits, which are essential companions for any meat or vegetable dish with juices that need sopping. In the buffet room at the Blue Willow Inn, biscuits are constantly being replenished.

We watched the Blue Willow cooks make them, and the one thing that impressed us was how *little* they handle the dough: the less kneading, the fluffier the biscuit.

2	cups self-rising flour
	Dash of salt
½	teaspoon sugar
3	tablespoons shortening
½	cup buttermilk
½	cup sweet milk
1	tablespoon water
1	tablespoon butter
1	tablespoon melted butter

Preheat the oven to 475°F. Sift the flour, salt, and sugar together into a mixing bowl. Cut in the shortening until the mixture is coarse. Add the buttermilk, sweet milk, water, and 1 tablespoon butter. Mix lightly until combined, but do not overmix. Pour the mixture out onto a floured surface. Knead the dough two or three times. (If biscuits are to be used for sandwiches, such as ham biscuits or other breakfast sandwiches, knead them a few extra times.) With floured hands, pat out the dough to approximately ½-inch thickness. Using a floured biscuit cutter or standard-size can, cut out the biscuits. Do not twist the cutter when doing this; press straight down. (Dough scraps can be rekneaded and cut, but biscuits from this cutting will be tougher, more suitable for sandwiches.) Place the biscuits on a lightly greased baking pan. Bake for 10 to 12 minutes, or until golden brown. Remove the biscuits from the oven, and brush them with the melted butter. Serve immediately.

MAKES 10 TO 12 BISCUITS

Buttery Biscuit Rolls

These rolls are another easily freezable breadstuff. If you plan on freezing them, remove them from the oven a few minutes early when they are only pale tan. Cool them completely, then seal them in plastic bags for freezing. To serve, thaw the rolls, then bake them at 350 degrees for a few minutes until golden brown. The Van Dykes suggest that you can add a tablespoon of dried herbs or two tablespoons of chopped fresh herbs (such as basil or rosemary) to the batter and give the rolls a flavor twist.

1   cup (2 sticks) butter or margarine
1   cup sour cream
2   cups self-rising flour

Preheat the oven to 350°F. Melt the butter in a large saucepan over medium low heat, whisking until completely melted. Add the sour cream and flour, and mix lightly. Spoon the batter into miniature muffin cups (do not grease), filling each one to the top. Bake for 15 minutes. Serve immediately. (Adding a tablespoon of dried herbs such as basil, rosemary, or 2 tablespoons of fresh chopped herbs to the batter makes a tasty addition to your meal.)

[Note: To freeze, remove the rolls from the oven several minutes early. Cool completely before freezing. To serve, thaw the rolls, and bake at 350°F for only a few minutes until golden brown.]

MAKES APPROXIMATELY 2 DOZEN

Cornbread Biscuits

Given to the Van Dykes by Mrs. W. D. Partee, this recipe makes biscuits that are ideal for crumbling atop a heap of collard greens or into a bowl of pot likker.

2	cups self-rising cornmeal
2	teaspoons baking powder
1	teaspoon salt
⅛	teaspoon baking soda
3	tablespoons solid vegetable shortening
1½	cups buttermilk

Preheat the oven to 475°F. Sift together the cornmeal, baking powder, salt, and baking soda. Cut in the shortening until the mixture is like meal. Add the buttermilk, and knead very lightly, only until mixed. Pour out onto a floured board, and roll out to about ⅓-inch thickness. Use a biscuit cutter to cut biscuits. Gently reroll the scraps, and cut more biscuits from them. Place the biscuits on lightly greased cookie sheet and bake for 12 minutes, until brown and slightly crunchy on the outside.

MAKES 12 TO 15 BISCUITS

BLUE WILLOW CHINA

"The Blue Willow Inn restaurant is popular not only because we serve food that Grandmother would have served," Louis Van Dyke said. "It's also because we serve it on Blue Willow china. Many of our customers remember that pattern on their everyday dishes growing up." To understand the importance of these memories, Louis explains, "Southern ladies cherish and value the china, dishes, silver, and linens that have been handed down from generation to generation. A true southern lady would more quickly part with her husband before parting with the family dishes."

Today you will find Blue Willow china in every corner, cabinet, and crevice of the Blue Willow Inn and beautiful examples for sale in the gift shop. Familiar as it may be to many of us Americans, the pattern has an unusual history and, if you know how to "read" it, an exotic love story to tell.

Its origins are English. It was first designed and engraved in 1780 by Thomas Minton, who sold it to Thomas Turner, manager of Shropshire Pottery, where it was mass-produced and eventually became the most popular china pattern in the world. Blue Willow has been imitated by Spode, Royal Worcester, Wedgewood, Davenport, and Leeds and Swansea. For two centuries the Blue Willow pattern has been in the repertoire of nearly every British china and porcelain maker.

When Thomas Minton designed it, artifacts from Asia were popular collectibles. His design illustrates the Chinese legend of a romance between Koong-se, daughter of a wealthy mandarin, and Chang, his lowly secretary. To keep the two young lovers apart, Koong-se's father erected a fence so they could not see each other; but the daughter found a way to contact her beloved anyway. She wrote a poem on a scrap of paper and placed it in a seashell, floating it down a stream to Chang.

Koong-se's father had promised her in marriage to a noble duke. Wearing a disguise Chang crept into the palace during the wedding banquet and eloped with Koong-se. Only at the last minute did the mandarin see them crossing a bridge, Koong-se carrying a box of jewels that were to have been her wedding dowry.

The lovers found a hideout with a maid who protected them, and later they moved to a distant island to spend their lives together. But time did not stop the mandarin's search. Eventually he found the couple and put them to death. According to the legend, God was so touched by their love that he immortalized Chang and Koong-se as two doves flying together in the sky.

If you look at a Blue Willow plate, you will see the elements of the story: the mandarin's palace, the bridge, the lovers running across to safety, the distant isle on which they settled, and two doves flying free in the sky.

Cornbread or Corn Muffins

There are two warm-bread drawers always filled in the buffet room of the Blue Willow Inn. On the top are biscuits. On the bottom are corn muffins. An essential element of almost any southern meal, corn muffins have a starchy sweetness that is an especially good complement to ham, pork chops, or streak o' lean.

	All-vegetable shortening
2	cups self-rising cornmeal
½	cup buttermilk
1	egg
1	tablespoon sugar
¼	cup plus 2 tablespoons butter or margarine, melted

Use the shortening to grease 15 cavities of a muffin tin or a baking pan. Preheat the oven to 350°F. Combine the cornmeal, buttermilk, egg, sugar, and the ¼ cup melted butter in a mixing bowl. Mix gently with a whisk, but do not beat. Pour into 12 to 15 cavities of the muffin tin or into the baking pan. Bake 15 to 18 minutes until golden brown. Remove from the oven, and brush the muffins or cornbread with the remaining 2 tablespoons melted butter. Remove the muffins from the tin, or cut the cornbread into squares and serve hot.

MAKES 12 TO 15 MUFFINS

Lemon-Sauced Gingerbread

It isn't necessary to serve this gingerbread with lemon sauce, but the sauce totally transforms it—from a sweet bread suitable for an afternoon snack into a blissfully warm dessert.

¾	cup brown sugar
¾	cup molasses
¾	cup melted butter
2	eggs, well beaten
2½	cups all-purpose flour
½	teaspoon baking powder
½	teaspoon salt
2	teaspoons baking soda
2½	teaspoons ground ginger
1½	teaspoons cinnamon
⅓	teaspoon ground cloves
1	cup boiling water

Preheat the oven to 350°F. Lightly grease and flour a 9 x 13 x 2-inch pan. In a mixing bowl combine the brown sugar, molasses, and melted butter. Add the eggs. Sift together the flour, baking powder, salt, soda, ginger, cinnamon, and cloves. Add to the sugar, molasses, butter, and eggs mixture. Mix well. Add the boiling water and mix thoroughly. Transfer the batter to the prepared pan, and bake for 35 to 40 minutes, or until a toothpick inserted in the middle comes out clean. Cool. If serving with Lemon Sauce (p. 178), serve the gingerbread and lemon sauce slightly warm.

MAKES 8 TO 10 GINGERBREAD SQUARES

Southern Dinner Rolls

Wonderful for freezing and using as needed when unexpected guests arrive. They'll think you've baked for hours. You have saved your "southern hostess hospitality" reputation once again.

1	cup shortening
1	tablespoon salt
½	cup sugar
2	cups boiling water
2	envelopes dry yeast
½	cup warm water
2	eggs, beaten
7	cups flour
	Vegetable oil

Combine the shortening, salt, sugar, and boiling water in a medium bowl, and mix well. Let the mixture stand until cool. In a small bowl dissolve the yeast in warm water, and add to the shortening mixture. Add the eggs, and mix well. Add the flour 1 cup at a time, and mix well. Grease the top of the dough with vegetable oil, cover, and refrigerate for 2 hours to let rise. Preheat the oven to 400°F. Roll the dough out on a floured surface to a ¼-inch thickness. Cut the dough into rounds with a 2-inch round cutter. Brush the top of each round with vegetable oil, then fold the rounds in half to form half-moons. Arrange the rolls on a baking sheet so the edges touch. Bake until brown. Serve hot, or let cool completely on a wire rack, and then freeze.

MAKES ABOUT 3 DOZEN ROLLS

Spinach Cornbread

Greens and cornbread go together as well as ham and eggs. This recipe, given to the Blue Willow Inn by Kitty Jacobs of Guidelines, Georgia, combines them in a luscious loaf that is moist, high-flavored . . . and good for you!

1	*(10-ounce) package frozen chopped spinach*
1	*(6-ounce) package Mexican cornbread mix*
½	*teaspoon salt*
½	*cup melted margarine*
¾	*cup cottage cheese*
1	*cup chopped onions*
4	*eggs, lightly beaten*

Preheat the oven to 400°F. Thaw the spinach well, and squeeze out as much moisture as possible. Place the drained spinach in a mixing bowl, and add the cornbread mix, salt, margarine, cheese, onions, and eggs. Mix well, and pour into a lightly greased, 8-inch-square baking dish. Bake 30 minutes, or until lightly browned. Allow to settle for 10 minutes before cutting pieces.

MAKES 16 (2-INCH) SQUARES

Spoon Bread

The name is a bit deceptive, for spoon bread is more like a cornmeal soufflé than any known piece of breadstuff. Although etiquette demands you eat it with a fork, it gets its name from the fact that it is served from the pan with a large spoon.

4	eggs, separated
2	cups milk
3	tablespoons butter
1	cup cornmeal
1	teaspoon baking powder
½	teaspoon salt
½	teaspoon cream of tartar

In a mixing bowl beat the egg yolks with an electric mixer at high speed until thick and light. In a saucepan over medium heat, combine the milk and butter. When hot, stir in the cornmeal, baking powder, and salt. When the batter thickens, remove from the heat, and gradually beat in the egg yolks. Preheat the oven to 375°F. In a medium bowl beat the egg whites with the cream of tartar until stiff. Gently fold the batter into the egg whites, and pour into a greased, 2-quart baking dish. Bake for 35 minutes, or until a toothpick inserted in the center comes out clean. Serve immediately with butter.

MAKES 8 SERVINGS

Sweet Potato Biscuits

Only slightly sweet, these biscuits make a fantastic companion for pork chops or ham. They should be served so hot from the oven that when they are split open and buttered, the butter melts right into them. If you have leftovers, use them instead of ordinary biscuits or bread as the secret ingredient in the best bread stuffing you've ever made!

2	*cups flour*
1	*teaspoon salt*
1	*teaspoon baking soda*
1	*tablespoon sugar*
⅓	*cup shortening*
1	*cup cooked, mashed sweet potatoes*
¾	*cup buttermilk*

Preheat the oven to 450°F. In a large bowl sift together the flour, salt, baking soda, and sugar. Cut in the shortening, and add the sweet potatoes. Stir in enough buttermilk to make a stiff dough. (You may need up to 1 cup or more.) Toss the dough onto a floured board, and knead lightly. Roll out to ½-inch thickness, and cut with a floured cutter. Bake until golden brown.

MAKES 12 TO 15 BISCUITS

Sweet Potato Bread

This is a simple, moist loaf that begs to be served warm with soft butter melting into it.

3	*large sweet potatoes*
4	*tablespoons vanilla*
1½	*cups flour*
4	*eggs*
2	*tablespoons cinnamon*
1½	*teaspoons nutmeg*
2	*cups sugar*
1	*cup milk*

Wash and peel the potatoes. Cover with water, and boil until cooked through. Drain off the water, and mash the potatoes, using a whisk or potato masher. Preheat the oven to 350°F. Combine the mashed sweet potatoes with the vanilla, flour, eggs, cinnamon, nutmeg, sugar, and milk. Mix well. Place in a large loaf pan, and bake for 20 to 25 minutes.

MAKES 1 LOAF

Yeast Rolls

Any worthy southern meal offers a breadbasket with not just one kind of bread. At the Blue Willow Inn, you can always count on corn muffins and buttermilk biscuits; but for mopping gravy, sometimes a soft yeast roll is essential.

1	*cup boiling water*
¼	*cup shortening*
¼	*cup butter plus melted butter for brushing tops*
⅓	*cup sugar*
1	*package active dry yeast*
1	*egg, beaten*
1	*teaspoon salt*
3⅔	*cups flour*

In a mixing bowl pour the boiling water over the shortening and the ¼ cup butter. When the butter and shortening have melted, stir in the sugar, and cool to lukewarm (about 105°F). Stir in the yeast, and let it dissolve. Stir in the egg and salt. Sift the flour into the liquid, about ¾ cup at a time, adding enough to make a soft dough. Lightly cover, and allow the dough to rise in a warm place for about an hour, until doubled in size. Punch down the dough, and form it into round rolls, each slightly bigger than a golf ball. Place these rolls on a lightly greased baking pan, and allow them to rise until doubled in size, about 30 minutes. Preheat the oven to 350°F. Bake the rolls for 10 to 12 minutes until lightly brown. Remove from the oven, and brush with the melted butter. Serve immediately.

MAKES ABOUT 2 DOZEN ROLLS

LUNCH, DINNER, SUPPER

Most people agree that eating three meals a day is a normal regime, but what those meals are called, particularly in the South, can be confusing. There is no misunderstanding about breakfast—that's what's eaten in the morning. And because it provides fuel for the working day, you can expect a southern breakfast to be large and full of calories: biscuits and sweet preserves, ham or streak o' lean, grits and gravy.

The midday meal is also a big one. Call it hot lunch, plate lunch, or meat-and-three. A noonday meal in the South is rarely a mere sandwich or salad. It provides an occasion to sit down with knife, fork, and spoon and tuck into a well-balanced menu of meat, vegetables, bread, and dessert, maybe soup and salad, too. That midday meal is known throughout the South as dinner because historically it was the biggest meal of the day, an opportunity to store up energy needed for the afternoon's hard work. Even in modern times, when most people don't pick cotton from sunup to sundown, the meal eaten in the middle of the day is known as dinner; and on holidays and special occasions, it remains the grandest of the three squares.

In the evening, southerners have supper, traditionally a lighter repast at the end of the workday. To dispel any confusion, the Blue Willow Inn (which does not serve breakfast) calls its midday meal lunch and its evening meal supper. The quantity and quality of dishes are the same both times of day, but it is interesting to see that it is at lunch, i.e., dinner, especially on weekends, when guests come to do their most serious pigging out. In the long shadows of the afternoon, it is not uncommon to see sated customers commandeer rockers on the front porch to snooze after the big meal known as dinner.

SANDWICH

and

SALAD

Chicken Salad

Good as a sandwich filling or, if the chicken is chopped especially fine, as the stuffing for hollowed-out cherry tomatoes.

3	cups cooked, chopped chicken
½	cup chopped celery
2	hard-boiled eggs, chopped
½	cup sweet pickle cubes
⅓	cup mayonnaise
	Salt

In a large bowl mix the chicken, celery, eggs, pickles, mayonnaise, and salt to taste. Refrigerate the salad for 1 hour before serving.

MAKES 8 TO 10 SERVINGS

Chicken Salad with Pecans and Grapes

The Van Dykes suggest this elegant chicken salad "for light luncheons and ladies' functions." They suggest serving it on a bed of lettuce with crackers on the side or stuffed into whole ripe tomatoes that have been wedged into a cup.

3   *cups cooked, chopped chicken breasts*
½   *cup toasted pecan pieces*
½   *cup white grapes*
⅓   *cup mayonnaise*
    Chopped celery (optional)

In a large bowl mix together the chicken, pecans, grapes, mayonnaise, and celery, if using. Refrigerate the salad for 1 hour before serving.

MAKES 8 SERVINGS

Pimiento Cheese

This recipe comes from Marvin Exley, Billie Van Dyke's foster father. The Van Dykes note that it is "a good addition to any refrigerator. It is great for fishing trips, hiking trips, excursions, and midnight snacks. It's also great for ladies' socials and soccer-mom snacks. Can be made into sandwiches, spread on Ritz crackers, or stuffed into celery ribs." For large families—or for large parties—the first version of this recipe yields about a gallon of pimiento cheese. The second version makes 5 to 6 cups. There would be no point in making less than that.

This is the recipe for large amounts of pimiento cheese.

---

3   pounds Cheddar cheese

3   (7-ounce) jars pimientos, diced and drained

3   (8-ounce) packages cream cheese

⅓   cup Worcestershire sauce

¼   cup mayonnaise

Grate the cheese, and place it in a mixer bowl. Add the pimientos and cream cheese. Mix at a slow speed. Slowly add the Worcestershire sauce and mayonnaise. After the mixture is consistent, increase the speed of the mixer until the consistency is smooth.

MAKES ABOUT 4 QUARTS

For smaller portions, use the following measurements:

1   (7-ounce) jar pimientos, diced and drained

1   pound (4 cups) Cheddar cheese

1   (8-ounce) package cream cheese

1   tablespoon Worcestershire sauce

2   tablespoons mayonnaise

MAKES ABOUT 5 TO 6 CUPS

Tea Sandwiches

With tea in the afternoon, you don't want a big piece of pie or cake; and yet a savory snack can seem too serious. These tea sandwiches are the perfect middle ground: sweet and fruity, elegant and satisfying. The Van Dykes suggest cutting the crustless white bread sandwiches into whatever shape you like. Traditional bite-size triangles work fine, but four good cookie cutters in the shape of playing-card suits will make them particularly appropriate for an after-bridge afternoon snack.

½	cup orange juice
1	tablespoon lemon juice
1	apple, cored and cut into small pieces
1	cup raisins
1	cup chopped pecans
	Dash of seasoning salt
	White bread, edges trimmed

In a food processor briefly blend the orange juice, lemon juice, apple, raisins, pecans, and salt to obtain a consistency that is easy to spread. Do not process the mixture until completely smooth. Spread it onto the trimmed bread, and cut it into desired shapes.

MAKES 3 TO 4 CUPS

The Perfect Ham and Cheese Sandwich

It is sometimes said that the difference between good and great is found in the details. Proof of that assertion is found in Louis Van Dyke's ham and cheese sandwich, the ingredients of which do not vary in any significant way from an ordinary ham and cheese sandwich. But as Louis once described it, "The important part is how the sandwich is layered to excite the taste buds. If it is just thrown together, it will not be the same." So, if you aim for perfection, disregard these exact ingredients and directions at your peril.

Kraft Miracle Whip salad dressing
Sandwich bread, white or whole wheat
Sliced ham
Kraft Deluxe Sliced American Cheese (Swiss may be substituted)
Iceberg lettuce
Juicy, big, ripe, red tomato
Prepared mustard
Salt and black pepper

Spread the Miracle Whip on each piece of bread. Place the ham on one piece of bread. Place the cheese on top of the ham. Add the desired amount of iceberg lettuce (use no other kind of lettuce). Place 1 or 2 slices of tomato on the lettuce. Spread the mustard on top of the Miracle Whip on the remaining piece of bread. Salt and pepper the tomato to taste. Close the sandwich, and serve it with potato chips. ("You'd better make two sandwiches, because you will not be able to stop with just one.")

MAKES ONE SANDWICH

ANN LOWE, HEAD COOK

I don't use recipes. I cook by taste," said Ann Lowe, who started work at the Blue Willow Inn on opening day and is now the head cook. "I make the vegetables and the casseroles and at least three meats. I taste everything."

Ann's mother cooked in a restaurant in nearby Covington for twenty-eight years, and much of what she knows, Ann learned as a child by watching. The first meal she cooked was a disaster: collard greens, cornbread, and candied yams. "I made them for my grandmother when I was nine, and they had no flavor, no flavor at all!" she remembered with a great laugh. When she was twelve she got a job washing dishes in the restaurant where her mother worked. "Pretty soon my mother showed me how to make chicken salad. I learned about seasoning, and after that, everything followed."

When Louis was opening the Blue Willow Inn, Ann had a job directing a child day-care center, but she was looking for part-time work. "All I wanted to do was something easy—washing dishes, maybe," she explained. "I had raised three sons, and I had cooked enough for them! I knew one thing for sure, and that was that I didn't want to cook any more! Just a little part-time job."

Ann's intention of finding something simple to fill her time was never realized, for she has become the heart and soul of the Blue Willow kitchen. She now arrives at the restaurant every morning around 7:30 and doesn't leave until midafternoon. And she doesn't just supervise; she hoists stockpots onto the stove, mashes potatoes, fries chicken, and chops greens.

Asked for some of her cooking secrets, she focused on vegetables, greens, and beans in particular, telling us that their secret was in the seasoning—fatback, bacon, and ham bones. "That's what makes these things southern," she explained. "It's the flavor of the pig." Ann continued: "Too many people put their salt and pepper in the pot in the beginning. I say you don't do it until it's done. That way, you can taste just what any dish needs. If you know the taste you're looking for, that's half the battle."

Another tip: "For yams, you need lots of sugar. That's where you get the nice glaze. And vanilla, for flavor."

Ann leaned close and whispered a secret she uses for hams to make them beautiful as well as delicious: a glaze of brown sugar and Coca-Cola. "You want a festive ham?" she asked. "Keep basting it with that Coke and brown sugar; and toward the end, you add your pineapples and cherries and baste them a little, too. I guarantee: It will be beautiful!"

Blueberry Salad

The term *salad* has multiple meanings on the southern table. It can be what it is to most other Americans, an assortment of leafy and low-cal vegetables, or it can be a gelatin concoction loaded with fruits, nuts, plenty of sugar, sour cream, and/or coconut shreds. This blueberry salad, a favorite of Billie and Louis's son Chip, is of the latter variety. "He enjoys it both as a salad and as a dessert," the Van Dykes note, suggesting that its color and its sweetness make it a wonderful thing to serve on special occasions.

1	(8-ounce) can crushed pineapple
1	(6-ounce) package blueberry or blackberry flavored gelatin
3	cups boiling water
1	(16-ounce) can blueberries, drained
1	(8-ounce) container sour cream
½	cup sugar
1	(8-ounce) package cream cheese, softened
½	cup chopped pecans

Drain the pineapple, reserving the juice. Dissolve the gelatin in boiling water. When thoroughly dissolved, stir in the pineapple juice. Chill until it is the consistency of unbeaten egg whites. Stir in the pineapple and blueberries. Pour into two 10 x 6 x 1-¾-inch pans, and chill until firm. In a bowl combine the sour cream, sugar, and cream cheese. Mix until smooth and well blended. Spread over the salad, and top with the pecans.

MAKES 8 SERVINGS

Buttermilk Congealed Salad

You won't likely come to the Blue Willow Inn without meeting Mae Morrow. She manages the restaurant and has been with Louis and Billie Van Dyke since they opened an earlier eatery in the American Legion hall in the nearby town of Monroe. On special occasions Mae uses her own gelatin mold, made personally by her, for the buffet room. It is true to southern food ways not only in its ingredients—notably buttermilk and chopped pecans—but in its title. Throughout the South gelatin molds go by the name of congealed salad.

1   *(8-ounce) can crushed pineapple, with juice*
1   *(3-ounce) package orange flavored gelatin*
2   *cups buttermilk*
1   *(6-ounce) package of refrigerated whipped topping*
2   *cups chopped pecans*

Drain the juice from the pineapple into a small saucepan. Add the gelatin, and cook over low heat, stirring until the gelatin is thoroughly dissolved. Cool. Mix the buttermilk and whipped topping. Add the pecans and gelatin. Pour into a mold or casserole dish, and refrigerate. Serve when firm.

MAKES 6 SERVINGS

Carrot-Raisin Salad

It seldom gets much attention because experienced eaters take it for granted (and often take second helpings), but carrot-raisin salad is as essential to the southern buffet table as cornbread.

8	to 10 large carrots, shredded
½	cup raisins
½	cup crushed pineapple
¼	cup mayonnaise
1	teaspoon sugar

Combine the carrots, raisins, pineapple, mayonnaise, and sugar in a mixing bowl, and mix well. Serve chilled.

MAKES 8 TO 10 SERVINGS

Coleslaw

Across this land there are as many kinds of coleslaw as there are styles of barbecue. Southern slaw tends to be sweet and a little tangy, making it a fine companion for spicy barbecued meats or fried chicken.

1	*medium head of cabbage, shredded*
¼	*cup shredded purple cabbage*
1	*heaping tablespoon sweet pickle relish*
2	*carrots, shredded*
⅓	*cup mayonnaise*
1	*tablespoon sugar*
1	*tablespoon white vinegar (optional)*
	Salt and black pepper

In a mixing bowl combine the cabbages with the pickle relish, carrots, mayonnaise, sugar, white vinegar, if using, and salt and pepper to taste. Stir well.

[Variation: Apple Coleslaw (great to accompany pork): Delete the pickle relish and vinegar from the above recipe. Cut two Granny Smith apples into small cubes. Do not peel. Combine with the slaw, and mix.]

MAKES 6 TO 8 SERVINGS

Cornbread Salad

Because cornbread is an expected staple at every Blue Willow meal, there always needs to be a good supply of it, hot from the oven. This means that frequently after meal time there is a surplus. One of the best things to do with extra cornbread, whether in loaf or muffin form, is to use it as the basis of this unusual salad, an item frequently found on the Blue Willow buffet tables.

8	cornbread muffins
1	(8-ounce) can green peas, drained
1	(11-ounce) can Mexicorn, drained
2	hard-boiled eggs, chopped
½	large bell pepper, chopped
½	large onion, chopped
¾	cup mayonnaise
	Salt and pepper

Crumble the muffins into a bowl. Add the peas, Mexicorn, eggs, pepper, onion, mayonnaise, and salt and pepper to taste. Toss lightly. Refrigerate, and serve cold.

MAKES 8 SERVINGS

Cottage Cheese Salad

"Cottage Cheese Salad" sounds kind of drab, doesn't it? Like something you'd have to eat on a diet. Of course, once you realize that this salad is served at the Blue Willow Inn, where deprivation eating is anathema, and that this is a true *southern* salad, it begins to sound a little more interesting. In fact, it is a good example of genuine Dixie-style home cooking (as opposed to the insipid versions represented by advocates of "new southern cooking"). It is an ambrosial expression of regional soul: ultrasweet, creamy, nutty, fruity, satisfying, and outrageously incorrect according to the abstemious standards of nutritional prigs.

---

1   (12-ounce) package cottage cheese (Please! NO low-fat)
1   (9-ounce) container refrigerated whipped topping
1   (10-ounce) can mandarin orange sections, drained
1   (20-ounce) can crushed pineapple
½   cup chopped pecans
1   (3-ounce) package orange-flavored gelatin

Combine the cottage cheese and whipped topping. Blend gently. Add the orange sections, pineapple, and pecans. Mix gently. Add dry gelatin, and mix. Chill.

MAKES 8 TO 10 SERVINGS

SOCIAL CIRCLE, GEORGIA

When you drive along the main street of Social Circle, you pass what appears to be a wishing well in a center island in the heart of town. Surrounded by flowers that the Social Circle Garden Club maintains, the small

Main Street, Social Circle, Ga.

gazebo has a plaque on it that describes the town's unusual name:

A group of men sitting in a circle, having their usual drink, were approached by a stranger. He was invited to join the group. Pleased with such hospitality, he exclaimed, "This is surely a social circle." This remark gave the town its name and this replica stands as a monument to this event.

Located at what was originally an important crossroads along the Hightower Trail east of Atlanta, the town was settled in 1820 and got its first postmaster in 1826. The Georgia Railroad made Social Circle Walton County's first rail center in 1845, and in 1848 a Masonic lodge was established.

When the town was incorporated in 1869,

its laws prohibited playing marbles on Sunday, disorderly horseback riding, tying horses to shade trees, and cock fighting. Any dwelling on a public street was required to be underpinned in such a way as to "keep out hogs and help abate the flea nuisance."

Social Circle today is a postcard-perfect small town where life seems slow and easy. It is especially beautiful in the spring, when the dogwood, wisteria, and cherry blossoms are in bloom. But any time of year, you can stroll along the main street and stop in the Claude T. Wiley Co. general store, an ancient wood-floored emporium with shelves of dry goods, groceries, and knickknacks. We were especially impressed by a collection of (not for sale) vintage soda bottles on one wall above a wooden plaque that advised *TRUST IN THE LORD*. We paid fifty-nine cents for a lovely lady's handkerchief and also bought a very practical denim jacket from the racks of work clothes.

Down the block and across the street are a number of shops, galleries, and antique shops and malls. Nancy Baldwin's Baldwin's Antiques has become one of Social Circle's gathering places for locals and visitors from afar.

Louis's Potato Salad

A man who likes to eat, Louis Van Dyke is anything but casual about casual foods. He has his own special way of preparing hamburgers (p.103) and hot dogs (p. 102) and is even persnickety about the proper method for assembling and cooking a grilled cheese sandwich (spread mayo inside the bread, with the cheese *before* grilling; and, if adding ham, grill it first, then cook the sandwich in the same ham-seasoned skillet). Similarly, his potato salad has a precise formula for something that tastes familiar and is no less than perfect. It's the platonic ideal of picnic potato salad.

6	medium all-purpose potatoes
3	plus 1 hard-boiled eggs
¼	cup chopped green salad olives
¼	cup mayonnaise
1	tablespoon prepared mustard
	Salt and pepper
	Paprika (optional)
	Fresh parsley sprigs (optional)

Peel the potatoes, and cut them into ½-inch cubes. Cover them with water in a stockpot, and bring the water to a boil. Cook until the potatoes are just beginning to test tender with a fork. Remove stockpot from the heat, drain, and bathe the potatoes in cold water to stop the cooking process. Coarsely chop the 3 eggs. In a mixing bowl, combine three of the eggs, olives, mayonnaise, mustard, and salt and pepper to taste. Mix gently, and transfer the potato salad to your serving bowl. Slice the remaining egg and arrange the slices on top of the potato salad. Garnish with a small amount of paprika and fresh parsley sprigs, if desired. Cover and refrigerate until serving.

MAKE 8 TO 10 SERVINGS

Waldorf Salad

"It's difficult planning a Thanksgiving menu because so much we set out on the buffet *every day* is like Thanksgiving," Louis Van Dyke says. "One thing we do for Thanksgiving is to expand the salad bar. Usually, we don't have such a large salad bar because the hot bar is so extensive and that is where people like to go. But Thanksgiving is a time when you expect something extra special, especially in the way of salads." Waldorf salad is one of the special-occasion dishes made at the Blue Willow Inn for Thanksgiving.

2	*cups diced apples (select hard, tart apples), washed with peel on*
2	*bananas, sliced*
¾	*cup chopped celery*
¾	*cup coarsely chopped pecans*
⅔	*cup raisins*
⅓	*cup mayonnaise*

If apples and bananas are not used immediately after dicing and slicing, toss them in ¼ cup of water with 2 teaspoons of lemon juice to keep them from discoloring. Mix together the apples, bananas, celery, pecans, raisins, and mayonnaise. Chill.

MAKES 8 SERVINGS

Watergate Salad

No back-of-the-box chef's repertoire is complete without a version of the opaque, pistachio-green mold made from either pudding mix or Jell-O, that somehow got known throughout the land as Watergate Salad. It was a favorite of Kim Unrah, who worked with the Van Dykes for many years and used to call it by the obvious name: Green Stuff.

1	*(3-ounce) package instant pistachio pudding*
1	*cup miniature marshmallows*
1	*(16-ounce) can crushed pineapple*
1	*(9-ounce) package refrigerated whipped topping*
⅓	*cup chopped pecans*

Mix together the pudding, marshmallows, pineapple, whipped topping, and pecans. Whip until fluffy. Refrigerate, and serve cold.

MAKES 6 TO 8 SERVINGS

Ambrosia Coconut

A special-occasion salad, ideal for Thanksgiving dinner, this is popular throughout not only the South, but also the Midwest where it is known as Millionaire Salad because of the luxurious nature of its ingredients.

---

2   *cups mandarin oranges, drained*

2   *cups crushed pineapple, drained*

2   *cups sour cream*

2   *cups shredded coconut*

2   *cups miniature marshmallows (white or multi-colored Funmallows)*

In a bowl combine the oranges, pineapple, sour cream, coconut and marshmallows. Chill.

MAKES 10 TO 12 SERVINGS

ROCKING CHAIRS

As a rule, it's hard not to like a restaurant that offers rocking chairs for the comfort of its customers. The chairs at the Blue Willow Inn are especially agreeable. Lined up on the front porch, they are big and broad, wide enough for the comfort of even an XXL person.

During warm weather, these chairs are available for sittin' and sippin' either before a meal or after. If you have to wait for a table (on weekends you likely will), one of the Antebellum Girls will be pleased to bring you a lemonade or iced tea to imbibe while you rock. What a joy it is to spend some time here. You feel like a southern aristocrat, surveying the broad front yard with its beautiful gardens and walkways, and the street that seems so very far away. You might say howdy to folks as they walk up the steps . . . or you might not say anything at all. The etiquette of rocking chairs does not require any conversation, with either those who walk past or with those rocking next to you. A pleasant hello is all that's mandated. Sitting on the front porch, swaying back and forth in anticipation of a great meal, or in the afterglow of one, is a private time to drift and to dream.

APPETIZERS

Chicken and Dumplings

Some first-time visitors to the Blue Willow Inn don't try chicken and dumplings, which is set out in the buffet room every day. The reason they disregard it is that the hot buffet table is so alluring and exciting, it draws them right away. Chicken and dumplings is on a side table, alongside whatever other soup is featured that day. It is indeed a soup; but it is as thick as stew and supremely comforting. A little goes a long way if you have an entire hot meal planned afterwards. At home, we have found that it makes a meal unto itself, especially for those times when comfort food is the order of the day.

1	(3 to 4 pound) chicken, disjointed
2	quarts plus ¼ cup water
2	cups self-rising flour
1	teaspoon salt
¼	cup shortening
½	cup melted butter
2	teaspoons black pepper

Combine the chicken and the 2 quarts water in a stockpot. Cook over medium-high heat until done, about one hour. Remove the chicken from the pot, reserving the broth. Cool the chicken in cold water. Remove the bones, skin, and fat. Cut chicken meat into bite-size pieces. In a mixing bowl, combine the flour and salt. Cut in the shortening until mixture is coarse. Add the ¼ cup water, and mix well with your hands. Bring the chicken broth back to a slow boil. With floured hands, pinch small quarter-size pieces of flour, and drop them into the simmering chicken broth. Gently stir after adding several pinches. Repeat until all the dumpling mix is used. Stir gently. Add the butter and black pepper. Simmer 8 to 10 minutes. Slowly stir in the chicken meat. Serve in soup bowls.

MAKES 8 TO 10 SERVINGS

Double-Oink Roll-Ups

It's no secret that pigs rule on southern menus. For breakfast, lunch, and supper, from streak o' lean to country ham and barbecue to Brunswick stew, pork is the meat of choice. That's a fact well reflected in these finger-food hors d'oeuvres, which combine a good mouthful of bacon and sausage in one piggy wallop.

¼	*cup butter*
½	*cup water*
1½	*cups herb-seasoned bread stuffing crumbs*
1	*egg, slightly beaten*
⅓	*pound bulk sausage, mild or hot to taste*
⅔	*pound bacon strips*

In a saucepan, melt the butter in the water. Remove from heat, and stir into the stuffing crumbs. Add the egg and sausage, and blend thoroughly. Chill for one hour, and shape into pecan-size balls. Preheat the oven to 375°F. Cut the bacon strips into thirds, and use these strips to wrap around the balls, securing each with a wooden pick. Place on a shallow baking pan. Bake for 35 to 40 minutes, turning once. Drain on paper towels. Serve hot.

MAKES ABOUT 30 ROLL-UPS

Chex Party Mix

"Party mixes can now be purchased in the grocery store," the Van Dykes note. But "none of them are the same as the traditional mixes prepared in home kitchens." Whether you consider this hors d'oeuvre retro chic or simply unchic, it is a cocktail-party classic every square-meals American cook needs to be able to make. "Whenever we bring out a bowl for friends, it vanishes faster than any other appetizer, except perhaps hot pigs in blankets," they declare.

1	*stick butter or margarine*
1¼	*teaspoons seasoned salt*
4½	*teaspoons Worcestershire sauce*
2⅔	*cups Corn Chex cereal*
2⅔	*cups Rice Chex cereal*
2⅔	*cups Wheat Chex cereal*
1	*cup salted mixed nuts*

Preheat the oven to 350°F. Heat the margarine in a large shallow roasting pan, about 15 x 10 x 2 inches, until it is melted. Remove the pan from the oven. Stir in the seasoned salt and Worcestershire sauce. Add the cereals and nuts. Mix until all pieces are coated. Return the pan to the oven, and cook about 1 hour, stirring every 15 minutes. Spread on a paper towel to cool.

MAKES ABOUT 10 CUPS

Crab Dip

Dips are the sociable hors d'oeuvre. As the prelude to a sit-down meal or as the main eating attraction at a stand-up cocktail party, a selection of dips, hot and cold, and a variety of crackers, chips, and crudités naturally encourage guests to intermingle as they eat. While guests at the Blue Willow Inn have little time for such frivolities—there is *serious* food to be eaten!—a catered party in Social Circle is rarely without at least a few of these dips to encourage mingling.

1	(8-ounce) package cream cheese, softened
3	tablespoons mayonnaise
1	teaspoon Dijon mustard
¼	teaspoon salt
2	tablespoons dry white wine
1	(8-ounce) can crabmeat, drained and flaked

In a double boiler combine the cream cheese, mayonnaise, mustard, and salt. Stir the mixture until smooth and well blended. Gradually add the wine. Then add the crabmeat and heat through. Serve the dip hot in a chafing or fondue dish with crackers.

MAKES ABOUT 2 CUPS

Deviled Eggs

"Every proper southern lady has a deviled egg dish for every occasion," Louis Van Dyke proclaims. "Deviled egg dishes are passed from generation to generation, often on the wedding day." Louis says that the minimum required egg dishes include a fine crystal dish for Sunday dinner and special occasions, theme egg dishes for Easter, Christmas, and Thanksgiving, and one Tupperware egg dish for such occasions as picnics, homecomings, tailgate parties, and the like.

7 *hard-boiled eggs, peeled*
2 *tablespoons mayonnaise*
½ *teaspoon prepared mustard*
1 *tablespoon sweet pickle relish*
   Salt and pepper
   Black or green olives cut in half, for garnish
   Parsley sprigs, for garnish
   Paprika (optional)

Cut six of the eggs in half lengthwise. Remove their yolks. In a medium bowl combine the yolks with the remaining whole egg, mayonnaise, mustard, pickle relish, and salt and pepper to taste. Mash well with a fork to blend the egg and yolks until smooth. Use a spoon to fill the cavities of the egg whites. Garnish each egg with half of a green or black olive and a sprig of parsley. Sprinkle lightly with paprika, if desired. Place in a deviled egg dish and serve cool.

MAKES 12 DEVILED EGGS

Dill Dip

One of the mildest condiments there is, Dill Dip is especially good when served with zesty crudités such as radishes or green onions.

1	cup mayonnaise
1	cup sour cream
1	tablespoon dill weed
1	tablespoon dried onion flakes or chopped green onions
1	tablespoon parsley
¼	teaspoon seasoned salt

In a medium bowl mix together the mayonnaise, sour cream, dill weed, onion, parsley, and seasoned salt. Chill the mixture before serving. This can be used as a vegetable dip with crackers or salmon croquettes.

MAKES 2 CUPS

Hot Artichoke Dip

The tang of chopped artichoke hearts and sharp cheese plus the creamy luxury of mayonnaise give this hot dip an irresistible poise that causes party guests to gather around and keep dipping until all the crackers are gone.

1½ *cups mayonnaise*
1¼ *cups plus ¼ cup freshly grated Parmesan cheese*
2   *(14-ounce) cans artichoke hearts, chopped and drained*
     Garlic powder
     Dash of Worcestershire sauce

Preheat the oven to 350°F. In a large bowl mix together the mayonnaise, 1¼ cups Parmesan cheese, artichoke hearts, garlic powder to taste, and Worcestershire sauce. Pour the mixture into a small casserole dish. Sprinkle the remaining ¼ cup Parmesan cheese on top. Bake the dip for 20 minutes, or until bubbly. Serve with party crackers.

MAKES ABOUT 5 CUPS

Oyster Dip

Although smoked oysters started their lives as fresh ones, their character is completely changed by the process that gets them flavored and in a can. You wouldn't want to substitute fresh ones in this classic dip recipe, for which the smoky, well-preserved nature of canned oysters is laced into sour cream and cream cheese to become a dip that is smooth and sultry at the same time.

2   (8-ounce) packages cream cheese, softened
1   teaspoon Worcestershire sauce
2   teaspoons lemon juice
1   cup sour cream
1   (3-½-ounce) can smoked oysters

In a large bowl blend together the cream cheese, Worcestershire sauce, lemon juice, and sour cream. Add the oysters and stir. Serve the dip with corn chips.

MAKES ABOUT 3 CUPS

Shrimp Wrapped in Bacon

A simple hors d'oeuvre, this combination of sweet and savory is about as luxurious as a bite-size piece of food can be. Good fresh shrimp and hickory-smoked bacon send it into the stratosphere.

Desired number of medium-size shrimp
French salad dressing.
As many full-size strips of bacon as there are shrimp

Peel and devein the shrimp. Marinate the shrimp 2 hours in the dressing. Preheat the oven to 350°F. Wrap each shrimp with a strip of bacon, and fasten it with a toothpick. Place the shrimp in a shallow pan, and bake for 10 minutes. Turn once; bake another 10 minutes. Drain on a paper towel, and serve immediately.

2 TO 3 SHRIMP PER PERSON

Stuffed Cherry Tomatoes

Along with deviled eggs, bread-and-butter pickles, and angel biscuits, stuffed cherry tomatoes are one of the necessary dishes for a ladies' luncheon, Social Circle-style. What's good about them is that they are dainty and pretty and require no utensils. Fine finger food!

Desired number of cherry tomatoes
Shrimp salad, tuna salad, or chicken salad (ingredients chopped fine)
Fancy leaf lettuce

Wash the cherry tomatoes. Hull out and discard the centers. Using a pastry bag or spoon, fill the center of each tomato with your favorite prepared salad. In order to get the tomatoes to stand upright, square off the bottom of each one with a sharp knife, removing only enough for the tomato to stay upright. Cover a serving dish with fancy leaf lettuce. Arrange tomatoes on the lettuce.

SERVINGS WILL DEPEND ON NUMBER OF TOMATOES PREPARED

Sugared Pecans

Sugary things are fundamental throughout the day and for virtually every course at the southern table, from peach preserves for morning biscuits to pecan pie for supper's dessert, with plenty of sweet tea in between. For a munchable snack to fill that bill, the Blue Willow Inn recommends sugared nuts, a recipe given to the Van Dykes by Margaret Hale.

2½	cups pecan halves
½	cup water
1	cup sugar
1	teaspoon cinnamon
1	teaspoon salt

Lay out a 3-foot sheet of waxed paper on the kitchen counter. Preheat the oven to 375°F. Heat the pecans on a cookie sheet in the oven for 15 minutes. Cook the water, sugar, cinnamon, and salt to a soft-boil stage. Do not stir. Add the nuts to the liquid, and mix well. Pour the nuts onto the waxed paper, and separate immediately. Cool before serving

MAKES ABOUT 3 CUPS

Sweet and Sour Hot Meatballs

These are great toothpick snacks to make for a buffet party, especially because they taste even better if made a day ahead, refrigerated overnight, and reheated. Word to the wise: don't use fancy or exotic grape jelly in this recipe. Regular Welch's is *de rigueur*.

2	pounds ground chuck
2	eggs, slightly beaten
½	cup bread crumbs
½	cup water
	Salt and pepper
	Garlic powder
1	(12-ounce) bottle chili sauce
1	(16-ounce) jar grape jelly
	Juice of 1 lemon

Preheat the oven to 350°F. Combine the ground chuck, eggs, bread crumbs, water, and salt and pepper and garlic powder to taste. Shape into meatballs the size of walnuts. Place on an ungreased cookie sheet, and bake for 15 to 20 minutes or until lightly browned. Drain off any grease. In a saucepan combine the chili sauce, grape jelly, and lemon juice. Bring to a slow boil. Add the cooked meatballs, and allow them to simmer 8 to 10 minutes. Stir gently so not to break up the meatballs. Serve hot in a chafing dish.

MAKES ABOUT 40 MEATBALLS

Virginia's Vidalia Onion Dip

Virginia is known for her wonderful parties and has the title of the best cook in the neighborhood. Her guests save room throughout the day to enjoy her enormous spreads. The men at her parties search out her Vidalia Onion Dip and scoop it by the spoonful. It is often said that Vidalia onions are so mellow that you want to eat one raw. Baking softens them and burnishes their natural sweetness even further; and when they are combined with cheese and mayonnaise and served warm, they become an unimprovable cracker dip.

2   Vidalia onions, chopped
1   cup grated Parmesan cheese
½   cup mayonnaise

Preheat the oven to 350°F. In a large bowl mix the onions, cheese, and mayonnaise. Bake in a casserole dish until bubbly. Serve with Melba toast or Ritz crackers.

MAKES ABOUT 3½ CUPS

VIDALIA ONIONS

You won't cry over a raw Vidalia onion. Slice into the firm, globular vegetable and it will bead with moisture, radiating aroma so appetizing that you want to eat it out of hand. And you can do that with a nice big Vidalia onion, just as happily as if it were a fresh-picked apple. With only a nice hint of onion's pungency, its overwhelming qualities are sweetness and crispness. It is exquisite raw – sliced thick to top the meat in a sandwich (or as the main ingredient of a sandwich, with mustard, mayo, pickle, and cheese!), slivered for a salad, or chopped as a garnish. You can pickle it, use it for soup, skewer it on the barbecue, or make it into onion rings; and when it is slow-baked, as served on the buffet table of the Blue Willow Inn, it becomes the most ambrosial earthy caramel.

Discovered by accident in 1931 when a Toombs County farmer named Mose Coleman realized that local soil produced onions that were uniquely flavorful, the crop was first sold at the farmer's market in the city of Vidalia. Because Vidalia is located midway between Macon and Savannah on busy Highway 280, the market became a favorite stop for travelers, who began to spread the word about the tasty onion being sold there. By the 1950s, Vidalia onions were available in supermarkets; and in 1990 the state legislature declared the Vidalia onion Georgia's official vegetable. By law, only onions grown in Southeast Georgia can bear the name Vidalia.

Late each Spring the city of Vidalia hosts a festival to celebrate the allium that has earned national and worldwide recognition. Events include a cook-off and an onion-eating competition, plus a beauty pageant to find the girl sweet enough to wear the sash that represents the most delicious onion of the South.

CELEBRATION
DAYS

CELEBRATION DAYS

Every meal served at the Blue Willow Inn is a gala feast, but holidays throughout the year attract greater-than-normal hordes of eaters and are the cause for extra-special menus. As at restaurants throughout the nation, Mother's Day is the biggest of them all, when up to seventeen hundred people will graze their way through the buffet line. No reservations are accepted on that day, and the wait for a seat can be as much as three hours. Likewise, Thanksgiving is huge. It is the one day of the year when there is a reservations-only policy. In almost all of December Thanksgiving-size meals are served to throngs of customers.

Here are Billie and Louis Van Dyke's notations and menu ideas for some of the special meals and traditions associated with the year's big holidays.

New Year's Day

A family day . . . and a big football day! Lots of snacks and beverages are required. The traditional New Year's Day dinner, served around noon, includes:

Apple salad
Roast pork (for good health)
Greens, turnip or collard (for prosperity), always seasoned with ham hock
Black-eyed peas with ham (for good luck), known as Hoppin' John
Candied yams
Rice
Cornbread
Biscuits
Lots of desserts
Sweetened iced tea and, for football watching, lots of cold beer

(Southern ladies always check with their men to find out the time dinner is to be served. Otherwise, if it is served during the game, the men will not join the dinner. Dinner must be served between football games.)

Valentine's Day

Always dress the table with a linen cloth and a lace overlay. Use candelabra and low lighting. Complement the table with fresh flowers. It is the gentleman's responsibility to bring the flowers, but subtle hints may be required.

A Valentine's Day menu would include:

Mixed greens salad with mandarin oranges and pecans, raspberry vinaigrette dressing
Beef tenderloin with roasted new potatoes
Green bean almondine
Heart-shaped yeast rolls
Chocolate cherry cake
Sweetened iced tea (the champagne of the South)

St. Patrick's Day

We are originally from Savannah, which has the second largest St. Patrick's Day celebration in America, after New York. Everyone becomes Irish on that day in Savannah. Ladies fill the beauty parlors to have their hair dyed green. When Louis was a teenager, his mother sent him to buy school shoes around this time of year, and although the family was on a strict budget, Louis bought green suede boots with metal buckles so he could wear them in the St. Patrick's Day parade. He did this knowing full well that if he wore them in the parade, they could not be returned to the store. He figured his mother would give him the money for another pair. Well, she was upset, but there was no more money for school shoes, so Louis wore green suede boots to school for the rest of the year and endured the taunts of classmates.

For most of us, St. Patrick's Day is an excuse to have an extra drink or two. Being conservative Protestants, we don't often get wild, but we like to drink "hairy navels" made of equal parts peach schnapps, vodka, and orange juice. And, of course, we make green potatoes and green biscuits and serve corned beef and cabbage.

Easter Sunday

First and foremost, Easter is a religious holiday in the South. Most southerners consider it the holiest day of the year. It is perhaps the only Sunday when chairs must be brought from the social halls into the sanctuary of the church to accommodate overflow crowds.

We don't eat much lamb here—we've tried to serve it, but customers aren't all that interested. Ham is the centerpiece, a big part of every Easter meal. The menu also includes:

Asparagus with Hollandaise sauce
Potato salad
Deviled eggs
Butter peas
Corn soufflé
Green beans
Easter cake: yellow with white icing with shredded coconut in the icing and decorated with jelly beans.

Easter Sunday is the South's answer to the runway fashion shows in Paris. While the men and boys are decked out in new suits, ties, and shoes, the ladies and girls are fashion statements, big time! Hats—the fancier, the better—are required attire. This applies to all females, babies to dowagers. Frilly lace, plumes, feathers, pastel colors, and flowers are all part of the outfit. No self-respecting lady would be seen on Easter Sunday in any attire she has previously worn, even if the weather is cold and rainy. Easter Sunday is the first day that any proper southern lady will appear in white shoes since Labor Day. This is the spring show!

Throughout the South, lawns are never cut on the Saturday before Easter so the grass will be high enough to hide eggs for Easter egg hunts. At the Blue Willow Inn, we have a "bunny" hiding eggs for the children all afternoon. Prize eggs are a favorite at the gift shop. Children win toys and stuffed animals.

Mother's Day

For our staff this is the most challenging day of the year. We bring in a horse and carriage to give rides to people who are waiting, as well as a clown or magician, or both to entertain. The wait is so well known that many customers bring blankets so they can sit on the ground outside and enjoy being a family together, a sort of picnic before the meal. Many have commented that their waiting time is a rare opportunity to visit with each other and not be bothered by telephones or television. We've got Antebellum Girls serving lemonade all day long, and we give candy-striped carnations to every mother.

This is not a day for mothers to stay home and cook for the family! It is a day to take Mother to her favorite restaurant. At the Blue Willow Inn, Chicken Divan (p. 116 and Orange Pecan Glazed Chicken (p. 127) are always Mother's Day favorites. Sometimes we do Cornish hens, and we always have extra salads, Jell-Os, and ambrosia. The mothers like those things.

Father's Day
We realize that most fathers would rather stay home and be cooked for, but there are certain things they especially like. We have fried catfish—that's the only Sunday of the year we serve it—and we borrow a huge charcoal grill to barbecue ribs by the pan. Fathers like big meals: Barbecued ribs and pork, fried catfish, meat loaf, mashed potatoes, and corn on the cob. They like pecan pie, peach cobbler, and always something chocolaty. Guys love Coca-Cola cake . . . and girls can eat it, too!

Independence Day
The Fourth of July is the only day of the year that southerners are Americans first and southerners second. Churning ice cream is part of the Fourth of July tradition. That's the height of peach season, so we'll be making fresh peach ice cream by the pool. We serve ribs and chicken and all the trimmings. Corn on the cob is just starting to come fresh in early July; and it is the one day of the year when we serve watermelon by the slice. The rest of the year, it's cubed.

Thanksgiving

In the South, Thanksgiving Day is the one day of the year that all the best silver, crystal, china, and linens are used. Serving pieces that are family heirlooms are brought out. Sunday manners and Sunday dress are essential!

Our Thanksgiving starts the week before when a group of us from the inn go to the Social Circle nursing home and feed them a big turkey dinner. Thanksgiving itself is family day at the inn, and it is so popular that we take reservations a full year in advance. The menu is traditional: roast turkey with cornbread dressing, sweet potato soufflé with miniature marshmallows melted on top or sweet potatoes with crushed corn flakes and pecans on top, creamed potatoes, giblet gravy, squash casserole, and, of course, macaroni and cheese.

After Thanksgiving, it's a must to have turkey sandwiches. The best way to make them is to use white meat on white bread with lots of mayonnaise, salt, and pepper. At the Blue Willow Inn, leftover turkey becomes Turkey Tetrazzini, Turkey Potpie, or Turkey Divan.

Christmas

We are closed Christmas Day, but our Christmas starts December 1. The decorations go up the day after Thanksgiving, and the whole month that follows is special. We have a lot of parties that time of year—offices, churches, families, ladies' groups—and it is the only time we serve the same thing every day: turkey, baked ham, roast beef, and fried chicken; collard greens, candied yams, green beans, corn pudding, butter peas, fried green tomatoes, cornbread dressing, giblet gravy, and—they'd scream if we didn't have it—macaroni and cheese. This is an important part of southern Christmas.

Sandi McClain, manager of the Blue Willow Inn gift shop, explains that on Christmas Eve in people's homes a casual menu is the order of the day. Early in the morning she prepares her sugar cookie dough so it can be refrigerated. The chili or Brunswick stew is made and put in the crockpot to simmer all day. In a second crockpot, the apple cider is brewed. While the Brunswick stew is simmering, there is time to put the finishing touches on Christmas gifts and to bake goodies for Christmas Day.

That evening, Sandi serves fresh fruit, Brunswick stew or chili, white bread and butter, sweet tea, and hot cider. For dessert, everyone comes together for rolling out the sugar cookie dough, each cutting his or her favorite shapes with a collection of cookie cutters. Then the competition begins! Laid out in front of everyone are every color of icing, sprinkles, and red hots. Each person is armed with a butter knife and his or her own creativity. By the last batch of cookies, everyone has the sugar crazies and eating another sugarplum is not an option.

Each child picks out a favorite decorated cookie to be left out for Santa with cold sweet milk.

Sandi says that a formal Christmas Day dinner would include: blueberry salad, beef tenderloin or crown rib roast, twice-baked potatoes, bean bundles, orange glazed carrots, yeast rolls, and sweetened iced tea. A variety of sweets is essential. These include: Carolina trifle, fruitcake, red velvet cake, pecan pie, and coconut cake.

Sandi also suggests the following recipe for a great Christmas breakfast casserole . . . just so long as you remember that it needs to sit overnight in the refrigerator before baking:

---

8 to 10 slices white bread, crusts trimmed
2 cups milk
6 eggs, beaten
1 pound sharp Cheddar cheese, shredded
1 pound hot pork sausage, cooked, crumbled, and drained
1 teaspoon dry mustard

Line a greased 9 x 13-inch baking pan with the bread. Combine the milk, eggs, cheese, sausage, and mustard and mix well. Spoon over the bread. Cover, and refrigerate overnight. Preheat the oven to 350°F. Bake for 45 minutes.

MAKES 8 TO 10 SERVINGS

Church Homecomings

Perhaps the best time and place for recipe swapping in the South is at a church homecoming. Once each year, most southern churches set aside a Sunday for this special occasion, to which all parishioners, past and present, are invited. Traditionally, a former pastor delivers the sermon, and afterwards all members and guests go to the church grounds for a grand picnic, to which everyone has brought their best and favorite dishes. It is customary for southern cooks to try to outdo one another in the splendor of the dishes they bring. There is recipe swapping galore ("except among those who closely guard their secrets," the Van Dykes point out); and after the picnic, the afternoon is spent on the church lawn singing gospel songs.

Funerals

In the South, when one goes to be with the Lord, it is referred to as "passing on." When there is a passing on in the family, the best friend is called to help. It is her role to coordinate all of the friends and church family in bringing food to the bereaved family's home. Many southerners keep a casserole in the freezer so it is ready when needed. The church of the departed frequently provides paper goods as well as spiritual support.

The proper foods include, of course, deviled eggs and fried chicken—classic southern comfort food. These are some of the meals traditionally brought to a grieving family's home:

> *Deviled eggs, fried chicken, mashed potatoes, and green beans*
> *Macaroni and cheese, biscuits, cornbread, and congealed fruit salad*
> *Baked ham, potato salad, peach cobbler, and a variety of cakes or pies*
> *. . . and always sweetened iced tea*

Bridge Club Luncheon

Sandi McClain's Aunt Frances is the grand doyenne of southern bridge ladies. She has been playing bridge since the age of six. And when she was seven, she and her ten-year-old brother filled in for a couple unable to make their usual appearance at their parents' bridge club. In this part of the world, bridge must go on!

Frances first joined her own bridge club when she was ten. One day when she and her little friends were meeting for a child's bridge luncheon and her mother was late coming home from the store, Frances went to the kitchen, found leftover congealed salad in the refrigerator, and served it to her friends with saltine crackers.

Her mother was horrified to come home and find that Frances had served food inappropriate for a bridge luncheon, so horrified, she remembers, that her mother nearly fainted!

Frances has been in the same bridge club with her friends since 1932. They meet twice a month. They begin playing at 10:30 A.M. and each lady puts fifty cents in the kitty for the day's winner. As with most southern bridge clubs, the ladies have a glass of wine during the last round before lunch. Some of the ladies like more than one glass, and some like quite a few. But it is the job of the group to make sure the bottle gets put away before anyone gets too tipsy. No wine is served after the last round before lunch; and bridge continues after lunch. Served in the dining room with good silver, crystal, fine china, and linens, a typical menu consists of frozen fruit salad, asparagus with ham, a brownie, sweetened iced tea, and coffee.

Bridge Luncheon Frozen Fruit Salad

2   *(3-ounce) packages of cream cheese, softened*

1   *cup mayonnaise*

1   *cup whipped cream (refrigerated whipped topping can be used; thaw and stir first to aerate)*

1   *(20-ounce) can crushed pineapple, drained*

1   *1/2 cups mini marshmallows*

1   *(6-ounce) jar cherries, diced*

1   *cup cut-up strawberries*

½   *cup blueberries or peaches (must be fresh, not canned)*

Combine the cream cheese, mayonnaise, whipped cream, pineapple, marshmallows, cherries, strawberries, and blueberries. Stir. Pour into a 9 x 13-inch casserole pan. Freeze. Cut into squares, and serve on a bed of lettuce.

MAKES 12 SERVINGS

Asparagus with Ham

4   *slices thin white bread (1 slice per person)*

2   *egg whites*

⅓   *cup mayonnaise*

12   *to 16 asparagus spears, fresh or canned, drained*

½   *cup Butter*

      Salt

4   *thick slices ham*

Toast the bread. Beat the egg whites stiff. Fold in the mayonnaise. In a pan with a little water, heat the asparagus with the butter and salt to taste. Drain the asparagus spears. Preheat the oven to 400°F. Lay the pieces of toasted bread on a cookie sheet. Place one piece of ham on each piece of bread. Place 3 to 4 asparagus spears on the ham. Place the egg white/mayonnaise mixture on top. Place in the oven, and cook until the topping turns brown. Remove from the oven and serve.

MAKES 4 SERVINGS

Aunt Frances's Brownie Recipe

¾   *cup all-purpose flour*

½   *teaspoon baking powder*

¼   *teaspoon salt*

1   *cup sugar*

2   *eggs, lightly beaten*

⅛   *cup butter, melted*

2   *squares of semi-sweet chocolate, melted*

½   *cup pecans, chopped*

1   *teaspoon vanilla flavoring or almond flavoring*

Preheat the oven to 350°F. Sift together the flour, baking powder, salt, and sugar. Add the eggs, butter, and chocolate. Add the pecans and vanilla or almond flavoring. Stir with a wooden spoon until the ingredients are mixed, but do not overmix. Pour into a greased 8 x 8-inch baking pan. Bake for 20 minutes. Turn off the heat before done, and let the brownies settle a few moments before removing them from the oven. Let them cool completely before cutting.

MAKES 16 (2-INCH-SQUARE) BROWNIES

Tailgate Parties

People have tailgate parties throughout the country, but in the South, tailgating is a way of life. Elsewhere, a tailgate party might consist of opening the back of the car, putting some meat on a grill, drinking a few cold beers, and listening to the radio. Participants arrive shortly before the game.

In the South, tailgaters begin arriving by 7:00 A.M. the day of the game, regardless of what time the game is to be played. Arriving early is fundamental. Parking spaces are valued commodities, and some groups who have tailgated together for twenty-plus years make sure that a designated couple arrives in plenty of time to secure "their" spots.

Once the tailgates are lowered, open tents are put in place and folding tables and chairs are set around. Grills, cookers, and ice chests are brought out. Lots of ice cold beer and bourbon are on hand to be consumed throughout the day. Someone is sure to bring a silver candelabrum to enhance one of the tables, especially at dusk.

Often adjacent groups of tailgaters join one another to eat and drink, and it is not uncommon for long-term friendships to develop. Southern tailgaters often attend fellow tailgaters' children's weddings, anniversaries, and funerals. It becomes a lifestyle, just like college football.

Probably the most famous tailgater in all the South was southern writer and humorist Lewis Grizzard. A graduate of the University of Georgia, he tailgated at Bulldog games for some thirty years. Since his death ten years ago, his tailgating spot has remained reserved and for every game, his chair is placed in that spot, and no one is allowed to occupy that space.

Here are a few typical southern tailgate menus, borrowed from a University of Georgia tailgating group:

Cold beer, BBQ chicken, BBQ pork, and BBQ ribs

Cold beer, hamburgers, hot dogs, potato salad, and chips

Cold beer, boiled peanuts (cooked on the premises), fruit salads, and fruits

Cold beer, deviled eggs, sweet gherkin pickle tray, and taco chips and hot sauce

Cold beer, pigs in a blanket, and country ham and biscuits (for early in the morning)

Cold beer with cakes, pies, and home-cooked desserts provided by the ladies

During the late summer, for the first games of the season, it is common to have fresh vegetables and fruit from the garden, such as corn, butter beans, okra, tomatoes, yellow squash, Vidalia onions, hot red peppers, new potatoes, watermelon, cantaloupe . . . and cold beer.

Teas and Receptions

Teas are an opportunity to wear one's Sunday best and practice one's "Emily" (Emily Post) manners. Many young girls as well as boys in the South attend manners camps or cotillion club classes where ballroom dancing and social graces are taught. Mothers of the South make sure that their sons and daughters will not embarrass their families.

And so, when a tea is given, usually to honor a young lady for a special event in her life, it is an opportunity for that education in good behavior to flower. Presents are not expected, but many teas have become a combination tea/shower where gifts are given.

A tea is a stand-up occasion where light finger foods are served with one's finest linen napkins, silver, and china. Pleasant small talk is a must.

Receptions are very similar to teas, but a reception will include gentlemen, whereas a tea is strictly for the ladies. Because men are invited to a reception, the food will be more substantial and generally include such items as boiled shrimp, sweet and sour meatballs, and chicken fingers, possibly even a carving station for meats. As is true of women at a tea, gentlemen at a reception are expected to wear their Sunday best, to display their Sunday manners, and to engage in pleasant conversation.

Appropriate occasions to host a reception include the introduction of a new member of the family (i.e., an engagement party), a celebration after such special occasions as a baptism or christening, the arrival of a new pastor or the departure of an old one, and the introduction of a new professional (doctor or lawyer) to the community. Some receptions are used as fund-raising events and may include a silent auction to support a worthwhile charity.

In the South, every reception has not only a purpose but a theme. For example, if an outgoing minister is being honored and he is an avid fisherman, the theme of the reception would be fishing.

Some food suitable for serving at teas and receptions includes fresh fruits in season (served in a carved watermelon basket), tiny tea sandwiches (perhaps cucumber and cream cheese), chicken salad in miniature puff pastry cups, hot Vidalia onion dip with crackers, hot artichoke dip with Melba rounds, cheese straws, roasted pecans, butter mints, Key lime squares, Jessica's raspberry nut bars, peppermint chocolate squares, tea, and coffee. A local favorite for receptions is this:

Magnolia Punch

2	*cups sugar*
2	*cups water*
1½	*cups orange juice*
¼	*cup lemon juice*
1	*(48-ounce) can pineapple juice*
3	*ripe bananas, mashed*
3	*quarts ginger ale*

In a large bowl mix together the sugar, water, orange juice, lemon juice, pineapple juice, and bananas. Freeze into a slush. Pour into a punch bowl, and add the ginger ale. Garnish with an ice ring made with orange and lemon slices and mint leaves. Garnish the punch bowl tray with magnolia leaves and flowers, if in bloom.

MAKES ABOUT 6 QUARTS

Bridesmaids' Luncheon

Bridesmaids' luncheons are usually given by a long-time friend of the mother of the bride, in a home, at a tearoom, or at a club.

The menu is usually light, such as chicken salad in cheese puff pastry shells, or tomato wedges with frozen salad served on a bed of lettuce, assorted minimuffins including cheese biscuits and blueberry muffins, deviled eggs, sweetened iced tea, and coffee.

With coffee, a beautiful dessert is always served, perhaps a bride's charm cake made with silver charms on satin ribbons that the bridesmaids pull to reveal a charm that symbolizes an activity or event in the bride's life. All charms are given to the bride to put on a charm bracelet as a keepsake of this special day. (Charm cakes are the work of professional bakers; don't try baking charms into your cake at home!)

The purpose of a bridesmaids' luncheon is to honor the bride's friends who are members of the wedding party. The bride selects a gift to give to each of them, usually jewelry that they will wear in the wedding, such as an engraved silver bracelet. During the luncheon, the bridesmaids are expected to share fond memories of the bride's growing up. Plenty of tissues must always be kept on hand as they will be needed for tears of joy.

The Blue Willow Inn is a popular setting for bridesmaids' luncheons and showers. Its southern charm and wide selection of food give guests choices for a memorable dining experience, and the inn has several small, intimate dining rooms that are perfect for these celebratory groups. Many bridal functions are also given at Magnolia Hall, the Blue Willow Inn's special-events facility. The stately white-columned Greek Revival mansion with beautiful gardens has been the setting of many luncheons and weddings. Brides often choose the Blue Willow Inn for their bridesmaids' luncheon, then after the luncheon, they walk to Magnolia Hall for the wedding rehearsal.

SIDE DISHES

Baked Pineapple Casserole

This treasured recipe was bequeathed to the Blue Willow Inn by Billie Harvey who, with her husband, sold the property to the Van Dykes. Mrs. Harvey used to bring it to church suppers and family gatherings in and around Social Circle. Until the Van Dykes "bribed" her to share it, the recipe remained her secret. This casserole fits especially well on a Blue Willow plate next to butter peas and ham.

1	(28-ounce) can crushed pineapple, with juice
1¼	cups sugar
2½	cups Ritz cracker crumbs
1	stick melted butter
2¼	cups grated cheese

Combine the pineapple and its juice with the sugar in a saucepan. Heat until the sugar is dissolved. Preheat the oven to 350°F. In a casserole or baking dish, layer the pineapple, cracker crumbs, butter, and cheese in three layers, saving the last ¼ cup of cheese to sprinkle over the top. Bake uncovered for 20 to 25 minutes until bubbly and golden brown.

MAKES 8 TO 10 SERVINGS

Baked Vidalia Onions

Baked onions are a delicious conundrum. They are absolutely beautiful in their pan on the buffet table, so beautiful that you always want one or two on your plate. These tender, cheese-frosted globes dress up dinner the way a top hat crowns a formal suit. And yet, the moment you lay knife or fork to one, it unravels all over your plate and looks a horrid mess. The good news is that the mess is entirely delicious, and its textural balance of silky-tender onion and crumbly cheese and croutons is sheer pleasure on the tongue.

6	*medium Vidalia onions*
½	*cup crushed croutons*
	Salt and pepper
½	*cup melted butter*
½	*cup shredded Cheddar cheese*
¼	*cup water*

Preheat the oven to 350°F. Peel the onions, and make two cuts diagonally across the top of each, cutting a little more than halfway down. Sprinkle the onions with croutons and salt and pepper to taste. Pour a small amount of the butter over each onion, using all the butter. Place the onions in a pan with water in the bottom and bake, uncovered, for 25 to 30 minutes (or in the microwave for 12 to 15 minutes) until tender. Remove from the oven, and top with the cheese. Return to the oven long enough to melt the cheese.

MAKES 6 SERVINGS

Black-Eyed Peas

Black-eyed peas are a familiar sight on the southern table, a good companion for country steak and mashed potatoes or a welcome fourth on an all-vegetable plate of collard greens, stewed apples, and okra. They are an essential dish for New Year's celebrations, as eating them will bring you good luck for the next twelve months.

2   *cups dried black-eyed peas*
    Water
2   *tablespoons bacon grease*
4   *ounces fatback (salt pork)*
4   *ounces ham or a ham hock*
    Salt and pepper

Place the dry beans in a pot and cover with water. Allow the beans to sit for one hour. Discard all the beans that float to the top. Rinse the beans three times with cold water. Put the beans in a stockpot and cover with water, at least two inches above the beans. Add the bacon grease, fatback, ham, and salt and pepper to taste. Cook the beans over medium heat, stirring often, for 1½ to 2 hours. Always make sure the beans are covered with water, adding water if necessary. Cook the beans until the juices are thick and the beans are tender.

MAKES 6 TO 8 SERVINGS

Broccoli Casserole

Like many children and other adults, we didn't think we liked broccoli . . . until we went south and saw what it can become. Given the royal treatment by Blue Willow cooks, the humorless vegetable is converted here into a flavorful green-lace casserole of cheese, eggs, and cracker crumbs.

2	*(16-ounce) packages frozen broccoli, or one bunch fresh broccoli*
1	*(10¾-ounce) can condensed cream of mushroom soup*
½	*cup mayonnaise*
1	*egg, beaten*
1	*cup plus ¼ cup grated Cheddar cheese*
½	*cup Ritz cracker crumbs*

Cook the broccoli until soft to the tooth. Drain, cool, and cut into bite-sized pieces. Preheat the oven to 350°F. In a large bowl mix the broccoli with the soup, mayonnaise, egg, and 1 cup cheese. Pour into a buttered 8 x 8-inch casserole dish. Top with the cracker crumbs, and bake for 30 minutes, or until bubbly. Sprinkle the remaining ¼ cup cheese on top, and return to the oven until the cheese is melted.

MAKES 8 TO 10 SERVINGS

Cabbage Casserole

In addition to the inevitable stream of visitors, you will see large numbers of regular customers at the Blue Willow Inn every Thursday. That's the day for liver 'n' onions (p. 126), a main course that is perfectly complemented by this drippingly good cabbage casserole. Billie Van Dyke first tasted it at a church supper, and she liked it so much that she lay in wait for the woman who made it to get the recipe for herself.

1	head cabbage, chopped
8	slices bacon
1	medium onion, chopped
1	medium green bell pepper, chopped
1	(10-¾-ounce) can condensed cream of mushroom soup
¾	cup grated cheese
½	cup milk
1	teaspoon salt
3	slices white bread, toasted and crumbled
1	stick butter, melted

Cook the cabbage for 8 minutes in salted water. Drain. Preheat the oven to 350°F. Fry the bacon in a saucepan until crisp. In the same saucepan sauté the onion and pepper until the onion is soft. In a large bowl combine the cabbage, bacon, soup, cheese, milk, and salt. Pour the mixture in a casserole dish. Toss the toasted bread in the melted butter, and spread it on top of the casserole. Bake for 35 minutes.

MAKES 6 TO 8 SERVINGS

SOUTHERN VEGETABLES

Southerners are crazy about vegetables. There are more vegetables on menus in the South than in any other region—squashes, tubers, peas, and pods that few Yankee cooks ever meet—and the variety available in markets and in restaurants is astonishing. Even the simple lima bean appears as a butter bean, a pole bean, a snap bean, and an October bean as the region's growing season proceeds nearly all year round. A salubrious essence-of-vegetable dish known simply as "greens"—might be collard greens, turnip greens, or mustard greens, each with its own distinct flavor and texture—is generally infused with the luxurious flavor of bacon drippin's, hambone, and/or fatback.

In few restaurants is vegetable passion more apparent than in the Walton Room of the Blue Willow Inn, where the buffet tables hold at least a dozen different vegetable dishes every day. We say "vegetable dishes" rather than merely "vegetables" because it is anathema to serve anything plain, except maybe tomatoes or sweet corn on the cob at the peak of their seasons. As a rule, southern-style vegetables are *not* for strict vegetarians because pork so often is used to enrich them. Broccoli is mixed not only with cheese and breadcrumbs, but frequently with shreds

of chicken to become the Blue Willow's Chicken Divan, or with chopped ham and noodles as a lavish casserole. Mild-mannered squash becomes a transcendent taste of goodness when flavored with bacon, cheese, Ritz crackers, and plenty of butter. Whole small Vidalia onions are crowned with cheese and crumbs and baked until

they virtually melt into fork-tender globes of sweet onion flavor. Butter peas look like traditional butter beans, but they are smaller and considerably more fragile than the usual legume, so soft they actually seem to caress your tongue. And instead of minuscule scraps of ham to flavor them, the serving dish contains large, lovely pink slices. (Be sure to have some of the pineapple casserole to complement this!) And of course, sliced green tomatoes are battered and fried to become crisp, tangy-lush discs, always accompanied by vividly sweet red tomato chutney.

According to Louis Van Dyke, the tradition of dolling up vegetables to attain maximum flavor goes back to the fact that so much southern cooking was a matter of making the most of paltry groceries. Neither tenant farmers nor slaves had the wherewithal to put beautiful hams and perfectly ripe tomatoes on their tables, so they used fatback from the hog to give such cheap vegetables as collards or pole beans a piggy wallop. And they fried green tomatoes to give them a crunch as opulent as a pan-fried chicken breast and a flavor beyond compare.

Furthermore, this kind of traditional southern cooking was enjoyed by hard-working people who required the energy of many carbs and calories to get through the day; so in addition to the gilding of butter, cheese, and breadcrumbs on vegetable dishes, the classic dinner spread abounds with sumptuous starches: escalloped potatoes, macaroni and cheese, potato cakes with bacon bits, cheese garlic grits, or glorified rice. "You can't have too many starches on the food line," is how Mr. Van Dyke explains his philosophy. "And some of them are essential. Whenever we put out escalloped potatoes, they get eaten well, but inevitably someone will ask, 'Where's the macaroni and cheese?' No meal at the Blue Willow Inn is complete without it."

Tops-All Cheese Sauce

A jar of Cheese Whiz makes all savories better. Here it adds silky texture and salty smack to a cheese sauce that the Van Dykes recommend for such dishes as seafood au gratin casserole and ham-potato casserole, and as a simple sauce to pour over cooked broccoli or into a just-baked potato.

¼	cup butter, melted
¼	cup all-purpose flour
2	cups milk
2½	cups grated Cheddar cheese
1	(16-ounce) jar Cheese Whiz
½	teaspoon salt
¼	teaspoon black pepper

Combine the butter and flour in a saucepan. Mix well over medium-low heat, stirring constantly to make a golden-brown roux. Preheat the milk in a microwave oven. Gradually add the milk to the saucepan, stirring constantly. Heat over medium heat. When hot (but not boiling), add the Cheddar cheese and Cheese Whiz. Continue to heat and stir until smooth and well blended. Bring to the lowest possible simmer, stirring often, for 5 minutes. Add the salt and pepper.

MAKES ABOUT 8 CUPS

Collard Greens

Before being cooked with ham hocks or salt pork, collards need to be washed and rewashed several times. Blue Willow collards are washed the old-fashioned way, by hand, before they are cooked until limp but still firm enough to provide a bit of tooth resistance, then chopped into leafy little pieces about the size of postage stamps.

Of all the vegetables served at the buffet line, Mr. Van Dyke may give the most thought to collards, which he calls "God's gift to the South." He says that they are always best when cooked a day ahead, chilled and reheated, a process that allows them to mellow and for the good pork flavor to thoroughly infuse the leaves. He also says that the best collards are those that have been through a frost while growing, thus becoming more tender. During the summer months, when frost-softened collards cannot be had, the Blue Willow puts its collards in the freezer for a few hours before cooking, thus "fooling" the leaves into softening as if they had survived a frost.

1	large bunch fresh collard greens
2	tablespoons bacon grease
½	teaspoon salt
1	tablespoon sugar
6	ounces fatback or a ham hock
¼	teaspoon black pepper
¼	teaspoon baking soda
1	quart water

Pull the leaves of the collards from the stems, and discard the stems. Coarsely chop or tear the leaves. Wash them thoroughly in cold water, changing the water several times. Drain. In a large saucepan combine the greens, bacon grease, salt, sugar, fatback, pepper, baking soda, and water. Boil slowly 2 hours or until tender.

MAKES 4 TO 6 SERVINGS

Cornbread Dressing

If ever you make cornbread muffins, or cornbread of any kind, don't worry about making too much. Leftovers are the foundation of a great side dish. Cornbread dressing (or stuffing, as it's known farther north) is the traditional companion to roast turkey or baked chicken; but there's nary a main course—fowl, meat, or fish—that isn't complemented by this Dixie classic.

½	cup chopped onions
¼	cup chopped celery
¼	cup butter or margarine
4	cups cornbread crumbs
2	cups biscuit crumbs
4	eggs, slightly beaten
2	hard-boiled eggs, shelled
½	cup chopped chicken or turkey giblets
1	teaspoon dried sage
2	cups chicken broth

Sauté the onions and celery in the butter or margarine in a small skillet until the onions are soft. Preheat the oven to 350°F. In a large mixing bowl combine the onions and celery with the cornbread and biscuit crumbs, beaten and hard-boiled eggs, giblets, and sage. Mix well. Add the chicken broth, and mix well again. Pour into a greased casserole or baking dish. Bake for 35 to 40 minutes, or until golden brown.

MAKES 8 TO 10 SERVINGS

Corn Pudding

Corn is an incredibly important part of southern cooking, from grits in the morning to pecan pie made from corn syrup for dessert. Throughout the warm part of the year, corn on the cob is eaten off well-set tables as well as picnic blankets. In cooler months, you can count on cornbreads, spoon bread made with corn meal, cornbread dressing to go with pork chops or turkey, and some kind of creamy sweet corn pudding. What follows is one of the all-time great recipes for corn pudding:

4	*eggs, beaten*
1	*stick melted butter*
1	*cup heavy cream*
1	*teaspoon salt*
⅓	*cup sugar*
½	*cup flour*
	Pinch of cayenne
2	*(16-ounce) cans creamed corn (do not use unsalted corn)*
2	*(10-ounce) boxes frozen corn niblets, semi-thawed*

Preheat the oven to 350°F. In a bowl mix together the eggs, butter, cream, salt, sugar, flour, and cayenne. Gently mix in the creamed corn. Add the corn niblets, taking care not to crush the kernels. Pour into an ungreased Pyrex or china baking dish, about 9 x 13 x 2 inches. Bake for 1 hour, or until the top is golden and the custard is set.

MAKES 8 SERVINGS

Creamed Potatoes

When Lewis Grizzard discovered the Blue Willow Inn and wrote a column to tell the world that he had found a southern culinary paradise, one of the points he made was that increasing numbers of restaurants have resorted to using instant mashed potatoes rather than making them the old-fashioned way. As far as Mr. Grizzard was concerned, the old-fashioned way is the *only* way!

How well we remember our first visit to the inn when we peeked into the kitchen at the height of lunch hour and saw the head cook, Ann Lowe, mashing a tub of spuds by hand with a heavy whisk. It is very hard work to plow through so big a mountain of potatoes, but the same result cannot be achieved by adding water to desiccated potato flakes or even by mashing potatoes with a machine. Here mashed potatoes are dense, buttery swells of ivory-hued delight, a significant presence on any plate.

6	medium potatoes
1½	quarts water
	Salt and pepper
¼	cup warm milk
⅓	cup melted butter
1	tablespoon mayonnaise

Peel and dice the potatoes. Bring the water to a boil in a large saucepan. Add the salt and pepper to taste and the potatoes. Boil until the potatoes are tender, about 15 to 20 minutes. Drain the potatoes, return them to the hot pan, and immediately add the milk, butter, and mayonnaise. Use a potato masher to mash the potatoes. Use a firm French whip to whip the potatoes until creamy. If they are too stiff, add a little more milk and butter.

MAKES 6 TO 8 SERVINGS

Fried Corn

When corn is fresh and sweet, there are few dishes more deeply satisfying than fried corn kernels. It takes some attention to properly cut the kernels off the cob. Use a sharp knife and take as much of all the kernels as possible but be careful not slice off any of the cob.

12	ears fresh corn
8	slices bacon
4	tablespoons butter
2	to 4 teaspoons sugar
2	teaspoons salt
¼	teaspoon black pepper

Cut the corn kernels from the ears, and place them in a bowl. Scrape the corn milk and remaining pulp from each ear, and add to the kernels. Cook the bacon in a heavy skillet until crisp. Remove the bacon and all but 2 tablespoons of bacon grease. Add the corn mixture, butter, sugar, salt, and pepper to the skillet. Cook over medium-to-low heat until the corn is tender and the mixture thickens. Stir often to prevent sticking. Serve in a vegetable bowl with crumbled bacon on top.

MAKES 8 SERVINGS

Fried Green Tomatoes

Culinary lore says that ripe red tomatoes felt so much like human skin that eating them was considered improperly erotic. In any case, there was something suspect about this New World member of the nightshade family that the Spaniards first brought back to Europe. One solution to its naughty nature was to eat green tomatoes, which are firm and not nearly as sweet as ripe ones. It is one item that is always set out at the Blue Willow buffet table, along with fried chicken and macaroni and cheese, and is the most popular dish in the house.

Fried green tomatoes are especially dear to the people at the Blue Willow Inn because it was this dish that made them famous.

2	*eggs*
1½	*cups buttermilk*
1	*tablespoon plus 1½ cups self-rising flour*
½	*plus ½ teaspooon salt*
½	*plus ½ teaspoon black pepper*
3	*large green tomatoes cut into ¼-inch slices*
	Vegetable oil for frying

In a bowl mix together the eggs and buttermilk. Whisk in the 1 tablespoon flour, ½ teaspoon salt, and ½ teaspoon pepper. Soak the tomato slices in this liquid. Whisk together the remaining flour, salt, and pepper. Heat about 1 inch of oil to 350°F in a heavy skillet. Dredge the tomato slices, one at a time, in the seasoned flour, shaking off any excess. Fry the slices in the hot oil; do not crowd. (Slices should not overlap as they cook.) Fry each side until it begins to turn brown. Turn in the oil and fry until golden brown and crisp. Drain on a paper towel. Salt to taste. Serve with tomato chutney.

MAKES 12 TO 15 TOMATO SLICES

Fried Okra

Ubiquitous on restaurant lists of vegetables available each day, fried okra is as addictive as snack food. While it is probably more polite to eat each marble-sized piece by spearing it with a fork, it is all too easy to pop one or two into your mouth by hand. Once you do that, you'll find yourself tossing them down the hatch two by two throughout any meal. While frozen okra works for gumbo (p. 135), fresh okra is essential if you are going to fry it.

2	pounds fresh okra
2½	cups cold water
1	cup plain cornmeal
1	cup all-purpose flour
	Salt and pepper
2	cups vegetable oil

Thoroughly wash the okra, and cut each piece into ½-inch lengths, discarding the ends. Pour the cold water in a mixing bowl, and immerse the cut okra in it to moisten. Mix the cornmeal, flour, and salt and pepper to taste. Heat the vegetable oil to 375°F in a large, heavy skillet. Drain the okra, and toss the pieces in the cornmeal/flour mixture. Place several pieces of okra into the heated oil (don't dump it all in at once). Cook until golden brown. Drain on paper towels.

MAKES 6 TO 8 SERVINGS

THE DAY LEWIS GRIZZARD CAME TO DINE

Around the Blue Willow Inn, the late Lewis Grizzard is considered to have been more than a fine southern writer and humorist. He was a miracle. In fact, he was the miracle that Billie and Louis Van Dyke had prayed for, although they didn't know when he walked in the door that their prayers were about to be answered.

After the inn opened in the fall of 1991, winter business was slow. It was a "destination" restaurant that few people knew about, nearly an hour's drive from Atlanta. In March, while in the Social Circle area for a photo shoot for the cover of his book, Grizzard found the Blue Willow Inn.

Louis Van Dyke knew Grizzard's writing and when he was told that the columnist was in the dining room, he went out to greet him. They talked about fried green tomatoes (of which Grizzard ate ten slices), the shame of those restaurants that serve mashed potatoes made from a box, and what makes a true southern meal. When Grizzard walked out the door, he said to Louis, "Watch the paper."

Two days later, his column in the *Atlanta Journal-Constitution* (and syndicated nationwide in three hundred newspapers) was headlined "Fried Green Tomato Hunt Ends at Blue Willow Inn." After describing the goodness of a meal of fried chicken, hot cornbread, sweet potato soufflé, baby lima beans, squash casserole, green beans, rice, and, of course, fried green tomatoes, Grizzard wrote, "I am a connoisseur of authentic southern cooking, which is getting more and more difficult to locate. Half the time when you think you've stumbled upon it, they serve mashed potatoes that come out of a box. But not at the Blue Willow Inn in Social Circle where every dish was authentic and delicious, including the banana pudding I had for dessert." The weekend after the column ran, the Blue Willow Inn made a profit for the first time. Within weeks, the bills were paid and the restaurant had become what the Van Dykes knew it had to be in order to succeed: a reason for people to travel many miles.

Later, when a side porch of the old Upshaw Mansion was enclosed and extended to become another dining room, the Van Dykes named it the Lewis

Grizzard Room. Today, the room's décor includes copies of Grizzard's best-selling books and an etched glass portrait of the man who did so much to put the Blue Willow Inn on the map.

(PHOTO COURTESY OF THE *ATLANTA-JOURNAL CONSTITUTION.*)

Green Beans

"In the South, Mama always canned green beans from the garden," Louis Van Dyke recalls. "That is why we always use canned green beans, even when fresh-from-the-garden are available. People come to the Blue Willow Inn to eat food like Mama or Grandmother made; so when it comes to beans, they have to be canned."

4	ounces fatback
4	ounces cooked ham or a hamhock
2	tablespoons bacon grease
¼	teaspoon brown sugar
1⅔	cup water
1	(28-ounce) can Italian-cut green beans
	Salt and pepper

Combine the fatback, ham, bacon grease, brown sugar, and water in a stockpot, and bring to a boil. Drain the juice from the green beans. Discard the juice, and add the beans to the boiling stock pot. Return the pot to a slow boil for 20 to 25 minutes. Add salt and pepper to taste.

MAKES 4 TO 6 SERVINGS

Grits Casserole

This is a savory side dish for almost any hot lunch or supper. Grits casserole is served every Friday and Saturday night at the Blue Willow Inn on the seafood/southern buffet.

4	cups water
1	teaspoon salt
¼	teaspoon black pepper
1	teaspoon garlic powder (optional)
1	cup quick-cooking grits
2	tablespoons butter or margarine
1	plus ½ cup grated Cheddar cheese
4	eggs, beaten
½	cup milk

In a large saucepan bring the water to a boil. Add the salt and pepper (and garlic powder, if desired). Gradually stir in the grits. Lower the heat, and simmer, stirring occasionally, for 5 to 7 minutes. Remove from the heat, and stir in the butter and 1 cup cheese. Preheat the oven to 350°F. In a small bowl mix the eggs with the milk, and add to the grits; stir. Pour the grits into a greased, 2-quart casserole dish. Top the casserole with the remaining ½ cup cheese. Bake for one hour.

MAKES 8 TO 10 SERVINGS

Macaroni and Cheese

The South is not unique in its love for macaroni and cheese, one of the true all-American comfort foods. At the Blue Willow Inn, it is one of the few items served *every* day, *every* meal.

---

1   (8-ounce) package macaroni

1   teaspoon vegetable shortening

¾   cup plus ¼ cup grated Cheddar cheese

½   cup Cheese Whiz

¾   cup milk

2   eggs, beaten

1   tablespoon mayonnaise

½   teaspoon prepared mustard

Salt and pepper

Cook the macaroni according to package instructions, adding the shortening to the water, and then drain. Do not overcook. Preheat the oven to 350°F. Combine the macaroni with the ¾ cup cheese, Cheese Whiz, milk, eggs, mayonnaise, mustard, and salt and pepper to taste. Bake uncovered in a 9 x 12-inch casserole (do not grease casserole) for 25 to 30 minutes. Remove from the oven, and top with the remaining ¼ cup cheese. Return to the oven only long enough for the cheese to melt.

MAKES 8 TO 10 SERVINGS

Mashed Potato Cakes

Here is a very good reason to make too many mashed potatoes. When Louis Van Dyke described to us how much he enjoys making potato cakes, his face lit up like a child about to get a present from Santa Claus himself.

¼   cup chopped onion

3   tablespoons bacon grease (and chopped bacon, if desired)

4   cups leftover creamed potatoes (p. 90)

1   cup flour

6   eggs
    Cooking oil

Sauté the onion in the bacon grease until soft. (Up to ¼ cup of chopped bacon may be added, if desired.) In a mixing bowl, combine the onion and bacon grease (and chopped bacon, if desired) with the mashed potatoes, flour, and eggs. Mix well, but do not beat. Pour enough oil into a heavy skillet to thoroughly cover the bottom. Form the potato mixture into patties ¾-inch thick and 2½ to 3 inches in diameter. Place the patties in the hot oil, and cook each side until golden brown. Add oil as needed while cooking the patties.

MAKES ABOUT 8 POTATO CAKES

Pecan Topping

Primarily used to crown a sweet potato soufflé, this topping is also delightful, slightly warm, on vanilla ice cream.

1	cup corn flakes
½	cup light brown sugar
⅓	cup melted butter
¾	cup chopped pecans

Crush the corn flakes into small pieces. In a mixing bowl combine them with the sugar, butter, and pecans and mix well. If using on a sweet potato soufflé, top the just-cooked soufflé with this mixture, and return it to the oven for 5 minutes to brown. If using to top ice cream, preheat the oven to 350°F. Spread it on a prepared cookie sheet, and bake it for 5 to 7 minutes, stirring so it doesn't stick or clump. Allow the topping to cool before spooning onto ice cream.

MAKES ABOUT 2 CUPS

Pinto Beans

Although pinto beans are the most common variety, the Van Dykes note that this same formula can be used for almost any other kind of dry bean, including lima beans, Great Northern beans, and white beans.

1	pound dry pinto beans
	Water
4	ounces fatback and/or ham
1	teaspoon bacon grease
	Salt and pepper

Place the dry beans in a pot, and cover with water. Allow the beans to sit for one hour. Discard all the beans that float to the top. Rinse the beans three times with cold water. Put the beans in a stockpot, and cover with water, at least two inches above the beans. Add the fatback or ham, bacon grease, and salt and pepper to taste. Cook the beans over medium heat, stirring often, for 1½ to 2 hours. Always make sure the beans are covered with water, adding water if necessary. Cook the beans until the juices are thick and the beans are tender.

MAKES 6 TO 8 SERVINGS

HOT DOG COOKERY

You won't find hot dogs on the Blue Willow buffet, except those days when the grade-school manners and etiquette classes come to visit. Even then, the little boys and girls don't get hand-food hot dogs. They get a casserole of franks and beans so they can practice their utensil skills.

Still, the Van Dykes have nothing against the all-American bunned hot dog. In fact, Louis offers several very practical tips for cooking and presenting one. Always using all-beef hot dogs, you can (1) put enough water in a small saucepan to cover the hot dogs and boil for 3 to 4 minutes; (2) microwave the hot dogs using medium power for 20 to 40 seconds per dog; or (3) grill the hot dogs on a charcoal grill. When grilling, turn the hot dogs frequently to prevent burning.

When using cheese on a hot dog, partially split open the dog when still very hot and fill the cavity with cheese. Place the hot dog back on the grill or in the conventional or microwave oven. Appropriate condiments include chili, sauerkraut, coleslaw, sweet pickle relish, ketchup, and mustard. Any or all of the condiments may be combined, except for sauerkraut and coleslaw. You can use only one of those two.

(Photo courtesy of the National Hot Dog & Sausage Council—www.hotdog.org)

HOW TO ASSEMBLE
A HAMBURGER

Just because hamburgers are not on the buffet at the Blue Willow Inn does not mean that Louis Van Dyke doesn't have an opinion about exactly how to serve one. He is one of those rare people who has an innate sense of what tastes good and looks appetizing, so when he talks, we listen. This is his advice for making a good hamburger:

A cooked hamburger should be juicy. Do not overcook.

If using a grill, toast the insides of the buns.

Spread mayonnaise on the inside of both the top and bottom bun.

Spread ketchup on the bottom bun.

Place the hamburger atop the ketchup.

Spread mustard onto the layer of mayo on the top bun.

Place lettuce atop the hamburger patty.

Place tomato and onion atop the lettuce.

Place pickle chips atop the tomato and onion. Close the bun.

(PHOTO COURTESY OF THE CATTLEMEN'S BEEF BOARD.)

Savannah Red Rice

A customary companion to seafood, Savannah red rice also looks mighty nice on a Blue Willow plate next to a slab of meat loaf, fried pork chops, or baked fish.

4	cups rice
6	slices bacon
1	medium onion, chopped
1	small bell pepper
1	(28-ounce) can tomatoes, mashed with a fork
1	(14-ounce) jar ketchup
1	teaspoon Worcestershire sauce
1	teaspoon salt
	Dash of black pepper
	Tabasco

Cook and drain the rice. Preheat the oven to 350°F. Fry the bacon until crisp and crumble it. Remove 2 tablespoons of the bacon grease from the pan for use in the casserole. Keep the remaining grease in the pan and sauté the onion and pepper until the onion is soft. Combine the rice, bacon, onion/pepper mix, tomatoes, ketchup, Worcestershire sauce, salt, pepper, and Tabasco to taste. Cook for 45 to 50 minutes, or until bubbly.

MAKES 15 TO 20 SERVINGS

Squash Casserole

Ann Lowe has been head cook at the Blue Willow Inn since it opened on Thanksgiving Day, 1992, and there is nothing on the menu that she can't (and does not) do well. When we asked her to name her favorite dish, she did not hesitate a moment before designating squash casserole. Often on the buffet table and impossible to resist if you've had it once, it is a Dixie tour de force in which an austere vegetable is the basis for an indescribably luxurious dish.

1	medium onion, chopped
2	tablespoons bacon grease
½	plus ¼ cup grated Cheddar cheese
½	teaspoon salt
1	(10 ¾-ounce) can condensed cream of chicken soup
1	cup sour cream
½	cup butter
3	eggs, slightly beaten
¼	cup chopped bacon
3	pounds sliced squash, cooked until firm
1½	cups plus ½ cup Ritz crackers, crumbled into crumbs

Sauté the onion in bacon grease. Preheat the oven to 350°F. In a mixing bowl combine the onion, ½ cup cheese, salt, soup, sour cream, butter, eggs, and bacon. Add the squash and 1½ cups cracker crumbs. Mix gently, but do not mash the squash. Pour into a 9 x 12-inch baking dish or casserole. Bake for 25 to 30 minutes. Remove from the oven, and top with the remaining ¼ cup cheese and ½ cup cracker crumbs. Return to the oven just long enough to brown the cracker crumbs and melt the cheese.

MAKES 8 TO 10 SERVINGS

Stewed Apples

Although sweet enough to be dessert (served warm with vanilla ice cream) or to serve as a filling for apple pie, stewed apples are frequently offered as one of several side dishes on southern menus. Like yams or stewed tomatoes, their sweetness makes sense as a complement to any kind of pork or chicken and as a counterbalance for bitter greens and tangy green tomatoes.

3	to 4 Granny Smith apples
1½	cups water
¼	cup brown sugar
2	tablespoons flour
¼	teaspoon salt
½	teaspoon cinnamon
¼	teaspoon nutmeg

Wash, core, peel, and slice the apples. Combine in a saucepan with the water, sugar, flour, salt, cinnamon, and nutmeg. Cook over low heat at a simmer for 30 to 40 minutes until the apples are tender, but not too soft.

MAKES 6 SERVINGS

Stewed Tomatoes

While fried green tomatoes are the Blue Willow Inn's signature dish (p. 92), every Southern cook has a reliable recipe for stewed tomatoes, too. Stewed tomatoes are totally different—not only from fried green, but from the kind of firm red beefsteaks used in salads and on sandwiches, different also from tomatoes as transformed into sauce for Italian food. Southern stewed tomatoes are luscious and goopy, usually at least a little sweet, and served as a kind of condiment for rice, creamed potatoes, or grits. Louis says his mother always served stewed tomatoes with mashed potatoes and fried fish. Their succulence—here underlined by the taste of bacon and a dash of sugar—is a reminder that tomatoes are in fact more fruit than vegetable.

1	(16-ounce) can whole tomatoes
2	slices bacon, cooked and chopped
1	tablespoon bacon grease
¼	teaspoon sugar, optional
	Salt and pepper
3	to 4 slices white bread

Pour the tomatoes with their juice into a small pot. Mash the tomatoes with a fork. Add the bacon, bacon grease, sugar, and salt and pepper to taste. Bring the mixture to a boil. Tear the bread into strips, and stir into the tomatoes. Remove from the heat, and serve over rice or creamed potatoes.

MAKES 4 TO 6 SERVINGS

Sweet Potato Soufflé

Sweet potatoes (also known as yams) are a fundamental element of nearly every hot lunch and supper throughout the South. In meat-and-three restaurants, where you order one meat and three vegetables off a written or posted menu, candied yams are always one of the choices. They are a presence at every good buffet, too; and the Blue Willow Inn is no exception. As tradition dictates, Blue Willow's sweet potato soufflé is flavored with vanilla and streaked with miniature marshmallows.

3   cups cooked fresh sweet potatoes, peeled if baked, drained if boiled
3   eggs
1   stick melted butter
½   cup whole milk
¼   cup light brown sugar
½   cup sugar
¼   cup raisins (optional)
¼   teaspoon cinnamon
1   teaspoon vanilla extract
     Dash of nutmeg
1   cup miniature marshmallows

Preheat the oven to 350°F. In a large bowl mash the sweet potatoes with a whisk or potato masher. Combine them with eggs, butter, milk, brown and white sugars, raisins (if using), cinnamon, vanilla, and nutmeg. Pour into a 9 x 12-inch casserole dish, and bake for 25 to 30 minutes. Top with the marshmallows, and return to the oven just long enough for the marshmallows to melt.

[Note: As an alternative to marshmallows, sweet potato soufflé can be topped with pecan topping on page 100]

MAKES 8 TO 10 SERVINGS

Tomato Chutney

Nothing complements fried green tomatoes as well as this sweet relish, which takes full advantage of the ripe tomato's fruity nature. It is vivid red, a beautiful contrast to the deep green color of the fried tomatoes inside their crust. This chutney is a great companion for almost any other fried, tangy, or savory food.

1	(16-ounce) can whole tomatoes
1	cup light brown sugar
½	cup sugar
2	cups finely chopped green pepper
1	cup finely chopped onion
2	tablespoons ketchup
2	to 10 drops Tabasco sauce
1	teaspoon black pepper

In a heavy saucepan stir together the tomatoes, brown and white sugars, green pepper, onion, ketchup, Tabasco, and pepper. Cook at a simmer for about 2 hours, stirring frequently until thickened. Cool. This will keep 2 weeks in the refrigerator.

MAKES ABOUT 6 CUPS

THE FIRST THANKSGIVING

The Blue Willow Inn served its first meal on Thanksgiving Day, November 26, 1991. "We fed maybe 125 people that first day," Louis Van Dyke recalls. "We ran ourselves crazy trying to keep those two-quart casseroles full and the Sterno cans lit under the household chafing dishes and just to make life interesting, our main stove quit working. Just quit! In order to keep it hot, somebody had to hold the pilot light button constantly, all day. We took turns doing it; I remember when my time came, I lay on the floor with my thumb on the button; I was so tired."

Billie Van Dyke recalls watching the waitresses carry iced tea to the tables, their hands shaking nervously. "I said to myself, *Dear Lord, please help those girls carry those glasses and not spill them.* That night when we went home, I cried and I cried. We were so tired; we were so broke; and I knew nobody would ever come back again."

Louis continues the story: "The day after Thanksgiving, we served Friday supper. Sixty-eight people came to eat . . . about four of whom were paying guests! You see, we had bartered meals for plumbing, painting, and electrical work to get this old house in shape; we had told so many people that if they did the work, we would give them meals. So we were feeding a lot of hungry people, but not making any money.

Those hard times are long past; and today Thanksgiving is an opportunity to remember just how far the restaurant has come. "Thanksgiving is so special to us here at the inn," Louis says. "In the morning the whole staff gathers in the foyer; we reminisce about the things that have happened over the years, and we say the Lord's Prayer. Then we get ready to feed fifteen hundred people."

MAIN COURSES

Ann Lowe's Feel-Better Chicken Stew

When head cook Ann Lowe needs to comfort a dear one, this is what she makes. It is a soothing soup/stew guaranteed to make anyone feel better, whether their ills are physical, mental, or spiritual. When Billie is feeling down or ill, a call always goes to Ann for chicken stew.

1	(2½ to 3½-pound) chicken
1	quart water
1	quart milk
1	cup butter
2	sleeves saltine crackers
	Salt and pepper

Wash the chicken thoroughly. Add to the water in the stockpot, and cook until tender. Remove the chicken, reserving the cooking liquid. Let the liquid cool slightly as you remove the skin and bones from the chicken, and tear the meat into bite-size pieces. Add the milk to the broth, and bring it to a slow boil, stirring frequently to avoid scorching. Stir in the butter. Crush the saltines, and add them to the pot. Add salt and pepper to taste. When the liquid thickens, add the chicken meat. Serve warm.

MAKES 8 TO 10 SERVINGS

Catfish Stew

The Van Dykes's recipe for catfish stew was inspired by Billie's foster father, Marvin Exley. Mr. Exley had a "shack" on Ebenezer Creek near Savannah, and whenever the family visited, he made his stew from catfish caught there.

1	pound bacon
1½	pounds catfish fillets
1½	cups chopped onion
4	cups diced potatoes
2	(16-ounce) cans tomatoes
⅓	cup tomato paste
2	tablespoons Worcestershire sauce
	Salt and pepper

Fry the bacon until crispy, and chop into small pieces. Cut the catfish fillets into bite-sized pieces. Remove the bacon, and fry the fish and onion in the bacon grease until fish are done and onion is tender. In a large pot combine the potatoes, tomatoes, tomato paste, Worcestershire sauce, and salt and pepper to taste, and bring to a boil. Cover the pot, reduce the heat, and simmer until the potatoes are tender. Add the fish, onions, bacon, and bacon grease into the mixture. Cover and simmer for another 20 minutes.

MAKES 12 TO 14 SERVINGS

Chicken Casserole

It isn't only because casseroles do so well on the buffet table that there are always several from which to choose at the Blue Willow Inn. The fact is that casseroles—of seasoned vegetables or of souped-up meat—are an essential element in the kind of southern cooking that evolved from slaves' soul food and poor white folks' farm kitchens. After all, a casserole is a way to stretch ingredients, to combine small amounts of groceries to make something big, and to create a dish that transcends its elements. This particular chicken casserole appears regularly in the buffet room. The recipe was a gift to Billie from Becky Young, the wife of Kenneth Young, former pastor of the Monroe, Georgia, Church of God. As is characteristic of so many true American casseroles from the East, West, North, *and* South, its multiple ingredients are bound together and infused with the flavors of canned soup. More distinctly Dixie is the inclusion of crumbled Ritz crackers.

1	cup sour cream
1	(10¾-ounce) can condensed cream of chicken soup
1	(10¾-ounce) can condensed cream of mushroom soup
1	cup chicken broth
8	chicken breasts, cooked and boned
2	stacks Ritz crackers, crumbled
1½	sticks butter, melted

Preheat the oven to 350°F. Mix together the sour cream, soups, and chicken broth. Place the chicken breasts in a baking dish. Pour the soup mixture over them. Top with cracker crumbs, and drizzle the crumbs with the butter. Bake for 35 to 40 minutes or until the crackers are well browned.

MAKES 8 SERVINGS

Chicken Divan

Having a party? Here's a dish that serves many and needs only a salad or relish to complete it. The recipe for Chicken Divan can be cut in half and is a perfect meal to make when you find yourself with leftover chicken (or, for that matter, turkey) and/or broccoli. It's a great combination of ingredients, but the secret that brings them all together, of course, is that casserole-chef's favorite flavor-enhancer, crumbled Ritz crackers.

2	(10 ¾-ounce) cans condensed cream of chicken soup
¾	cup mayonnaise
⅔	cup milk
2½	cups plus ⅓ cup grated Cheddar cheese
3	tablespoons concentrated lemon juice
1	tablespoon curry powder
3	pounds cooked broccoli
3	pounds cooked, boneless chicken
2	cups crumbled Ritz crackers

Preheat the oven to 350°F. In a large bowl combine the soup, mayonnaise, milk, the 2½ cups cheese, lemon juice, and curry powder. Mix well, but do not beat. Layer a casserole or baking pan with the broccoli, then the chicken. Spread the sauce mixture over the chicken. Add the cracker crumbs. Bake for 30 to 40 minutes. Remove from the oven, and top with the ⅓ cup grated cheese. Return to the oven only long enough for the cheese to melt. Serve hot.

MAKES 10 TO 15 SERVINGS

Chicken Tetrazzini

It has an Italian name, but chicken Tetrazzini—named for internationally famous Victorian-era coloratura soprano Luisa Tetrazzini—reassures eaters around the globe. It combines those twin mainstays of the comfort food pantheon, chicken and noodles; and in this case, creamed soup and Cheez Whiz.

1	(8-ounce) package vermicelli noodles
1	quart chicken broth
¼	cup coarsely chopped green peppers
¼	cup coarsely chopped onions
½	cup sliced mushrooms
1	heaping tablespoon pimientos
¼	cup chopped black olives
3	tablespoons butter
1½	cups chicken, cooked and deboned
½	cup milk
¼	cup Cheese Whiz
1	(10-¾-ounce) can condensed cream of chicken soup
½	plus ¼ cup grated Cheddar cheese

Cook the noodles in the chicken broth, according to package directions. Sauté the peppers, onions, mushrooms, pimientos, and olives in the butter. Preheat the oven to 350°F. Combine the chicken, noodles, sautéed vegetables, milk, Cheese Whiz, chicken soup and the ½ cup cheese. Pour the mixture into a 10 x 13-inch casserole dish. Bake for 30 to 40 minutes or until bubbly. Top with the remaining ¼ cup cheese, and return to the oven just long enough for the cheese to melt.

MAKES 12 SERVINGS

Country-Fried Steak

Like the fried meat Texans know as chicken-fried steak, country-fried steak can be ornery or delectable. Done right, it is one of Louis Van Dyke's favorite meals—a dish he ate at least once a week when he was growing up. Now it is a regular in the entrée rotation at the Blue Willow Inn. Unlike its Texas cousin, which is customarily served with pepper-cream pan gravy, this country steak comes with gravy that is augmented by a can of creamed soup.

¼	cup cooking oil (minimum)
½	medium onion, sliced
6	(4-ounce) portions cubed beef steak
½	cup flour
½	teaspoon salt
¼	teaspoon pepper
1	(10¾-ounce) can condensed cream of mushroom soup
½	cup water

Cover the bottom of a large heavy skillet with the cooking oil. Turn to medium heat, and sauté the onion until tender. Remove the onion, and set aside. Use a meat mallet to tenderize the steaks. Combine the flour with the salt and pepper. Dredge the tenderized steaks in the seasoned flour. Fry each side of each steak in the oil in the skillet 4 to 5 minutes over medium heat. Add more oil if needed. Remove each steak from the skillet to drain on paper towels. Add the cream of mushroom soup and water to the skillet, and cook over medium heat, stirring often.

[Note: There are two alternative methods for finishing the steaks: (1) Return the steaks to the gravy in the pan, place the reserved onions on top, and turn the heat to low. Cook for 15 to 18 minutes or (2) Preheat the oven to 350°F. Place the cooked steaks in a casserole dish, and pour the gravy over them. Cover with onions. Cover the casserole, and bake for 15 to 20 minutes. Serve with mashed potatoes.]

MAKES 6 SERVINGS

Fatback and White Gravy

In this day and age of nutritional priggishness, we are thrilled that a dish named "fatback" still exists! Also known as streak o' lean (although lean it ain't!), it is something like bacon taken to the nth degree: as luxuriously porky as food can be.

½	to 1 pound fatback or streak-o-lean
2	tablespoons flour
1¼	cups milk
	Salt and pepper

Slice the fatback into ¼-inch-thick slices. In an iron skillet cook the fatback over medium heat, turning to cook both sides. Cook the fatback until golden brown and crisp. Remove the meat from the skillet. Reserve 2 tablespoons of the drippings in the skillet. Add the flour to the drippings, stirring with a whisk or fork until smooth. Add the milk and cook, stirring until desired thickness. Add the salt and pepper to taste. Pour over the fatback and enjoy.

MAKES 4 TO 6 SERVINGS

Fried Catfish

Catfish is almost always served in abundance. Those restaurants that make it a specialty frequently offer it on an all-you-can-eat basis: pay one price and plow through all the catfish, hushpuppies, and sweet iced tea you desire. Such plenty is always the case, with every dish, at the Blue Willow Inn, which is why no specific amounts are given for the number of catfish used in this recipe. The rule of thumb is: make a lot!

Desired number of (4 to 8-ounce) catfish, cleaned and ready to fry
Water
Salt
Cooking oil
Self-rising cornmeal

Place the catfish in cold water, adding ½ teaspoon of salt for each pound of catfish. Heat the cooking oil in a heavy skillet, using enough oil to cover the catfish. Remove the catfish from the water, and dredge it in the cornmeal, completely covering the fish with the cornmeal. (Salt can be added to the cornmeal if desired). Place the fish in the oil, cooking each side for 6 to 10 minutes, depending on the size of the catfish. Drain on paper towels.

SERVINGS DEPEND ON NUMBER OF CATFISH

Fried Pork Chops with Pan Gravy

Fried pork chops are a taste of pure-pig-pleasure. If the chops are thick enough, their insides stay moist and succulent while the exterior turns crisp; and when the chops are done, you make savory gravy from the drippings in the pan. With stewed apples, mashed potatoes, and greens on the side, this is the anchor of a grand southern feast.

6	(5 to 6-ounce) center-cut pork chops
1½	cups plus 3 tablespoons flour
	Salt and pepper
	Cooking oil
¼	cup water

Wash the pork chops in water. Combine the 1½ cups flour and salt and pepper to taste. Dredge the pork chops in the flour mixture. Pour enough oil in a heavy skillet to cover the bottom. Turn the heat to medium. Place the pork chops in the skillet, but do not crowd them. Cook until the red juices are showing on the top of the chops. Turn the chops over, and add a little more oil to prevent them from sticking. Cook for 8 to 10 minutes more until the chops are golden brown and the insides are no longer pink, but they are still moist. Remove the chops from the pan to make the gravy.

To make the gravy, add the water and 3 tablespoons flour to the drippings in the skillet. Cook over medium heat, stirring constantly and scraping any bits and pieces of the pork chops from the bottom of the skillet. Add a little more water if the gravy gets too thick; or sprinkle in more flour if it is too thin. Cook over low heat for 10 to 15 minutes, stirring frequently. Serve the gravy as a side dish to ladle over the chops, or return the chops to the skillet, and smother them with the gravy.

MAKES 6 SERVINGS

BUFFET STRATEGIES

Joyful though it may be, dining at the Blue Willow Inn requires difficult decision making. For those lucky enough to be able to come to the inn a few times every week, or even once a week, the dilemma isn't so critical; but for visitors from afar, for whom a meal here is a rare occasion, the problem of choosing exactly what to put on one's plate, and how much of it, can be a kind of delicious torture.

In the Walton Room buffet in the center of the inn, you are confronted by a modest salad table, a soup table, a dessert table, and a sweeping U-shaped buffet where the hot meats and vegetables are arrayed. It is a visual knockout punch. To inhale the soothing aroma of hot chicken and dumplings (a regular on the soup tray), the pickly tang of green tomatoes, and the piggy opulence of fried pork chops is a ravishing experience. But be warned: no matter how big an appetite you are packing when you arrive, it is absolutely impossible to have a satisfying serving of everything that tempts you.

With four to six different entrées and at least a dozen vegetables on display, not to mention biscuits and cornbread and relishes and puddings and salads and umpteen pies, cakes, cookies, brownies, and cobbler, you must make a basic choice. Aim for a tiny bite of everything you like or take plenty of your favorites and miss out on dozens of good things to eat. If one craves a good-sized portion of skillet squash, does that mean there will be no room on the plate for this kitchen's superlative macaroni and cheese? Must you ignore the cornbread dressing in order to save a spot for sweet corn casserole? If you come to the Blue Willow Inn craving a feast of baked and smothered pork chops, then you likely won't even have a chance to appreciate the kitchen's magnificent streak o' lean (thick strips of bacony pork that vary in texture from wickedly

crusty to meltaway-lush, blanketed with smooth white gravy).

Of course, everyone is welcome to return to the buffet for second, third, fourth, and fifth helpings—clean plates are provided for the return trips—but the predicament is that some dishes are so darn delicious that you want to pile your plate with them again and again, recklessly sacrificing variety for monomaniacal satisfaction.

It is fascinating to observe customers' strategies in this regard. One day we watched a woman heading from the buffet room toward her table carrying a plate with nothing but vegetable casseroles and soufflés; another focused even more precisely, piling her plate with three kinds of beans. One man sidestepped vegetables altogether and walked away from the buffet toting a plate teetering with fried chicken pieces, slabs of meat loaf, and a mountain of smothered steak. A white-haired couple dressed in matching running shoes and lavender windbreakers zeroed in on the serving tray of fried green tomatoes and piled two plates high with nothing but the golden-fried discs and a few dabs of chutney, grinning ear to ear as they toted their treasure back to their table.

"We have two rules here," a waitress warned us the first time we sat down at the beginning of a Blue Willow Inn meal. "Rule one is that no one goes home hungry. Rule two is that everybody has to have at least two desserts." She then clued us in to an insider's way of stocking up: "When it's time for dessert, ask me for supper plates." The dessert table is stocked with small bowls of which you can take as many as you please, but a full-size plate allows for two or three pieces of cake per serving.

Grits Lasagna

Is this American southern or southern Italian? It is a melting-pot meal, that's for sure. It is a reminder that while the South, and southern cooks in particular, honor tradition, one important element of that tradition has always been to use what's available to make something good to eat. In this case, common grits take the place of more exotic lasagna noodles, and American cheeses are used in place of European ones. And don't get creative with the tomato sauce: Ragu brand is essential. The result is a dish based on the layered principle of Italian lasagna, but with a purely American and very southern character.

7	cups water
1	teaspoon salt
2	cups quick-cook grits, uncooked, or 2 cups instant polenta, uncooked
1	pound lean ground pork (not sausage)
1	cup chopped fresh mushrooms
1	(30-ounce) jar Ragu Thick & Hearty spaghetti sauce
1½	cups shredded sharp Cheddar cheese
1½	cups shredded Monterey Jack cheese

Bring the water and salt to boil in a large saucepan. Gradually add the grits, stirring constantly. Reduce the heat and simmer, stirring all the while, for 5 minutes, until the grits are thick and pull away from the sides of the pan. Pour the grits into a 15 ½ x 10½-inch jelly roll pan or sided cookie sheet, spreading evenly to cover the bottom of the pan. Let stand 30 minutes until cool and firm. Cut the grits into approximately 3-inch squares. Preheat the oven to 450°F. Cook the ground pork in a large skillet until browned, stirring to crumble. Drain. Combine the pork, mushrooms, and spaghetti sauce. Mix well. Arrange half the grits squares in the bottom of a 13 x 9 x 2-inch baking pan coated with nonstick spray. Spoon half the sauce over the grits, spreading it to the edges. Sprinkle on half the cheeses. Repeat to create a second layer. Bake for 15 to 20 minutes or until hot and bubbly. Let stand 10 minutes before serving.

MAKES 10 TO 12 SERVINGS

Ham Broccoli Noodle Casserole

While there can be no avoiding the fundamental entrées that anchor the Blue Willow buffet—fried chicken, pork chops, meat loaf—it is impossible not to become smitten by the meat-based casseroles. They are beautiful, unusual, complex, and deeply southern. They remind us of the kind of super-duper dishes that a good home cook would prepare for a church homecoming, when the order of the day is to bring your best. This ham-broccoli-noodle casserole is luxurious and colorful. With a spoonful of tomato chutney on the side, it's a plateful of pleasure.

½   cup mayonnaise

2   cups broccoli florets, fresh or frozen (defrosted)

1   cup plus ½ cup shredded sharp Cheddar cheese

1   cup chopped ham

1½ cups macaroni or corkscrew noodles, cooked and drained

2   tablespoons finely chopped green bell pepper

¼   cup milk

½   cup seasoned croutons

Preheat the oven to 350°F. In a medium bowl mix together the mayonnaise, broccoli, 1 cup of the cheese, ham, noodles, bell pepper, and milk. Spoon into a 9 x 12-inch casserole dish. Sprinkle with the remaining ½ cup cheese and the croutons. Bake 25 to 30 minutes, until bubbly.

MAKES 6 TO 8 SERVINGS

Every-Thursday Liver and Onions

Not too many people cook liver at home any more; there is at least one member of every family who can't stand it! Just the same, there is likely a member of that same family who loves liver and onions. If that's the case, and that family is in driving range of the Blue Willow Inn, you might see them at the buffet table on Thursday. Liver and onions is always one of the half dozen entrées set out Thursday for lunch and for supper. If it weren't there, Louis would no doubt hear serious complaints from the large contingent of liver lovers who count on this recipe once every week.

Cooking oil
Thinly sliced onion
Desired number of pieces of beef liver
Salt and pepper
Flour

In a heavy skillet, pour a small amount of cooking oil, and turn the heat to medium. Sautée the onion slices until tender, soft, and slightly brown. Remove the onions from the skillet and set aside. Add salt and pepper to taste to the flour. Coat each side of the liver pieces with the seasoned flour. Pour enough oil in the skillet to cover the bottom. Place the liver in the hot oil. When red juices are flowing from the top, turn the liver. Add a little more oil if needed to keep the liver from sticking. Cook for 2 to 3 minutes more, and turn again. Do not overcook: this makes the liver tough. When done, remove from the heat, and serve smothered with the onions.

SERVINGS WILL DEPEND ON THE NUMBER OF LIVER SLICES PREPARED

Orange Pecan Glazed Chicken and Wild Rice

Mother's Day is extra special at the Blue Willow Inn, and one dish that is always set out on the Mother's Day buffet is Orange Pecan Glazed Chicken. "Women love it," Billie Van Dyke said. "It's a good dish for any special occasion or holiday meal."

1	(6-ounce) package Uncle Ben's Long Grain & Wild Rice
	Chicken broth as needed
1	cut-up chicken
3	tablespoons plus 1 tablespoon melted butter
	Salt and pepper
½	cup orange marmalade
¼	cup frozen concentrated orange juice
1	teaspoon cornstarch
½	cup chopped pecans

Cook the rice according to directions on the package, using chicken broth instead of water. Preheat the oven to 350°F. Place the chicken on a baking pan. Baste with the 3 tablespoons of butter, and season with salt and pepper to taste. Bake the chicken for 25 to 30 minutes. In a saucepan combine the 1 tablespoon butter, marmalade, and orange juice. Bring to a boil. Dissolve the cornstarch in a small amount of water. Slowly stir in enough of the cornstarch to thicken the butter/orange mixture. Add the pecans. Place the cooked rice in a 9 x 13-inch casserole dish. Arrange the baked chicken on top of the rice. Pour the orange glaze over the chicken. Return to the oven, and cook for 12 to 15 minutes, or until glaze begins to brown.

   [Note: Cornish game hens can be substituted for chicken. Either cut the hens in half lengthwise or cook whole.]

MAKES 6 TO 8 SERVINGS

Magic Baked Pork Chops

"I seldom go to food shows," Louis Van Dyke admits. "I am not looking for new ideas. I don't want any shortcuts." For example, he wouldn't think of making mashed potatoes from anything but peeled, boiled potatoes. Forget boxed, instant spuds! On the other hand, there are certain *shortcuts* that have become part of the southern cook's repertoire and are as true to culinary custom as an Easter ham. When green beans are on the table in most southern homes and restaurants, they are canned, not fresh, for the simple reason that fresh green beans cannot hold up to the long cooking times demanded if you are going to have them sop up enough flavor of the fatback to make them delicious. Furthermore, canning beans is a venerable kitchen activity of which any good grandma would approve.

One of the most familiar shortcuts used by cooks throughout the nation, especially by those in the South who favor casseroles and creamy meat dishes, is the use of canned soup. In this Blue Willow recipe, one can of Golden Cream of Mushroom soup—a brawny brew thick with mushroom slices—elevates pork chops from something good into something deluxe. Easy? You bet! Traditional? Every bit as much as whipped topping on dessert.

6	center-cut pork chops
1	(10¾-ounce) can Golden Cream of Mushroom Soup
⅔	cup water
	Pepper
	Garlic salt

Preheat the oven to 350°F. Lightly grease a casserole dish. Place the pork chops in the dish, and cover them with the soup; then add the water. Cover the dish, and cook for 30 to 40 minutes, until the chops are cooked through. Add pepper and garlic salt to taste.

MAKES 6 SERVINGS

Pork Tenderloin

This recipe was contributed to the Blue Willow kitchen by Elton Wright, the inn's former business manager who is now retired. It's a good example of just how sweet and succulent pork can be. Serve it with greens on the side.

1	pork tenderloin, cut in half lengthwise
2	tablespoons yellow mustard
2	teaspoons thyme
1	teaspoon ground ginger
1	teaspoon salt
½	teaspoon minced garlic
½	teaspoon black pepper
½	cup port wine
¼	cup soy sauce
2	tablespoons vegetable oil
¼	cup currant jelly

Place the halved tenderloin in a rimmed pan barely big enough to hold it. Mix together the mustard, thyme, ginger, salt, garlic, and pepper. Spread the mixture over the tenderloin. Mix the port wine and soy sauce. Pour this over the tenderloin. Cover the tenderloin, and refrigerate for 24 hours. Remove the tenderloin from the refrigerator, and reserve its marinade. Heat the vegetable oil in a heavy skillet. Brown both sides of the tenderloin, starting with the fat side. Remove the tenderloin from the skillet (reserving drippings), and place it on a roasting pan sprayed with nonstick vegetable oil. Preheat the oven to 375°F. Combine the marinade with the drippings in the skillet, and pour this over the meat. Cook the meat covered for about 5 minutes per pound. Uncover and cook an additional 7 minutes per pound. Combine the drippings from the roasting pan with the currant jelly, and serve as a condiment for the meat.

MAKES 6 TO 8 SERVINGS

Pot Roast with Gravy

"A meal in itself," the Van Dykes note. "Or it can be served with rice."

1	(6- to 8-pound) beef rump roast
¼	teaspoon garlic salt
3	potatoes, peeled and diced (approx. 1-inch pieces)
4	carrots, peeled and cut into 1-inch pieces
3	ribs celery, cut into 1-inch pieces
1	onion, sliced
2	cups water
	Salt and pepper
	Flour

Preheat the oven to 350°F. Sprinkle the roast with the garlic salt. Combine the potatoes, carrots, celery, and onion. Place the roast in the center of a roasting pan. Spread the vegetables around the roast. Add the water to the pan. Salt and pepper the vegetables to taste. Cover and bake for 45 to 55 minutes. Remove the cover, and cook for another 15 minutes.

For the gravy, combine the drippings from pot roast with ¼ to ½ cup water in a small skillet. Over medium heat add the flour to thicken. Simmer, stirring frequently. If the gravy is too thick, add more water. If it's not thick enough, add a small amount of flour. The gravy can be poured over the pot roast or served as a side dish.

SERVES 10 TO 12

Red-Eye Gravy with Ham

Our favorite explanation for how this gravy got its name is based on the fact that black coffee and ham drippings never totally mix; and if you pour the coffee into the ham drippings nice and easy, it will spread out in the hot fat and resemble a very bloodshot eye! In any case, no serving of country ham is complete without it. Whether it comes in a pitcher alongside for spooning onto the ham or in a puddle on the plate *with* the ham, its unctuous nature is an ideal foil for the salty smack of the long-cured pig meat. The Van Dykes recommend drizzling some on freshly baked open-faced biscuits and grits.

3	*slices country ham, about ¼-inch thick*
¼	*cup strong coffee*
¼	*teaspoon sugar*

In a large iron skillet fry the ham slices on each side. Remove the ham from the skillet. Add the coffee and sugar to the ham drippings. Stir to blend over low heat. Return the ham to the skillet, and simmer in the gravy until hot. Great served with open-faced biscuits—homemade, of course.

MAKES ABOUT ½ CUP

Reliable Meat Loaf

If it's Thursday at the Blue Willow Inn, you can count on meat loaf. Some customers make a regular habit of Thursday dinner because they like the meat loaf that much. Also frequently served on Sunday, this is a substantial, beefy loaf that demands good whipped potatoes and greens on the side.

1½	pounds ground chuck
3	eggs
½	plus ½ cup ketchup
1	cup corn flakes
3	leftover biscuits or 5 to 6 slices of white bread
¼	cup chopped green bell pepper
¼	cup chopped onion
1	tablespoon Worcestershire sauce
	Salt and pepper

Preheat the oven to 350°F. In a large mixing bowl combine the ground chuck, eggs, ½ cup ketchup, corn flakes, biscuits, bell pepper, onion, Worcestershire sauce, and salt and pepper to taste. Mix well, and pour onto a sheet pan. Work several times as if kneading bread. Mold into a loaf, and place into a lightly oiled loaf pan. Bake for 30 to 40 minutes. Remove from the oven, and top with the remaining ½ cup ketchup. Return to the oven for 5 to 7 minutes to glaze the ketchup. Allow the loaf to rest for 10 to 15 minutes before slicing to serve.

MAKES 10 TO 12 SERVINGS

Sausage and Gravy

Also known as Hoover gravy (from Depression days), sausage and gravy is a natural companion for hot biscuits and grits.

1	pound pork sausage, cut into rounds
1	tablespoon all-purpose flour
¾	cup milk
¼	cup water
	Salt and pepper

In an iron skillet over medium heat, cook the sausage, turning once. Pour off all but two tablespoons of sausage fat and any pieces of sausage from the skillet. Add the flour, and stir with a fork or wire whisk until it has browned. Slowly stir in the milk and water, and cook until the desired thickness. Season with salt and pepper to taste. Serve the gravy in a gravy boat with the cooked sausage.

MAKES 4 TO 6 SERVINGS

Savannah Shrimp and Rice

Savannah is where Billie and Louis Van Dyke grew up and where they learned to eat and to cook. Their coastal flair is especially evident on Fridays at the Blue Willow Inn, when the buffet includes seafood galore. One of the most deluxe dishes is this favorite of Billie's from a recipe given to her by a neighbor on Burnside Island.

1	small onion, chopped
1	small green pepper, chopped
1	tablespoon butter
8	cups cooked rice
1	pound cooked shrimp, peeled and deveined
1	(10-¾-ounce) can condensed cream of mushroom soup
¼	teaspoon curry powder
	Salt and pepper
½	plus ¼ cup grated Cheddar cheese

Sautée the onion and pepper in the butter. Preheat the oven to 350°F. In a mixing bowl, combine the onion and pepper with the rice, shrimp, soup, curry powder, ½ cup grated cheese, and salt and pepper to taste. Mix well. Pour shrimp mixture into a 9 x 12-inch baking dish. Bake for 25 to 30 minutes until bubbly. Remove from the oven, and immediately sprinkle the remaining cheese on top. Serve hot.

MAKES 8 SERVINGS

Seafood Gumbo

On Friday and Saturday, you pay a little extra to eat at the Blue Willow Inn because the vast buffet features all-you-can-eat seafood. Among the Van Dykes's favorites is this coastal classic.

1	cup chopped celery
2	cups chopped onions
1	green bell pepper, chopped
3	tablespoons butter
1	pound fresh or frozen okra
3	quarts water
2	(16-ounce) cans tomatoes
1	(12-ounce) can tomato sauce
	Tabasco Sauce
2	pounds shelled and cleaned shrimp
1	pint raw oysters
1	pound crab meat
	Salt and pepper
	Cooked rice

In a large, heavy skillet, sauté the celery, onion, and chopped pepper in the butter until the onion is soft. Add the okra, and continue stirring until the okra is tender. In a 6-quart stockpot combine the water, tomatoes, tomato sauce, and Tabasco sauce to taste. Cook over medium heat for 30 minutes. Add the sautéed vegetables, and continue cooking over low heat for two hours, stirring occasionally. Add the shrimp, and cook 15 minutes more. Add the crab meat and oysters, and cook 15 minutes more. Season with salt and pepper and additional Tabasco sauce, if desired. Serve over hot rice.

[Note: for thicker gumbo, dissolve 1 to 2 teaspoons of cornstarch in 1 tablespoon of water and add to the pot, stirring to thicken.]

MAKES ABOUT 5 QUARTS GUMBO

Southern-Fried Oysters

The goodness of fried oysters depends on two things: the batter and the oysters themselves. If you use small- to medium-sized oysters with a sweet ocean taste, fresh as can be, this dish sings. The batter in which they're dipped works also for scallops and shrimp.

Vegetable oil for frying
1   *cup self-rising cornmeal*
1   *cup self-rising flour*
¼   *teaspoon red hot pepper (optional)*
2   *eggs*
2   *tablespoons milk*
24 *ounces fresh select oysters, drained*

In a deep skillet or fryer, heat the vegetable oil to 375°F. Combine the cornmeal, flour, and pepper, mixing well. Combine the eggs and milk, mixing well with a fork. Dip the oysters in the egg mixture; then dredge them in the flour mixture. Fry them in the vegetable oil for 2 to 3 minutes, or until golden brown. Do not crowd the pan. Drain the cooked oysters on paper towels, and serve immediately.

MAKES 4 TO 6 SERVINGS

THE Fried Chicken

Louis Van Dyke is a fried chicken fanatic. "I order fried chicken everywhere I go, even in a Chinese restaurant," he says. "So I was fussy when I developed the recipe for the fried chicken we serve here at the Blue Willow Inn. It is simple, and it works!" It is grand and true southern fried chicken, nearly greaseless, but with a well-spiced crust that has a luscious texture, shattering at first bite and infusing the meat within with flavor. It is one of the dishes that is *always* on the hot buffet, lunch and supper, every day of the week.

1	chicken, cut into 8 pieces
1	quart water
1½	cups flour
½	teaspoon salt
½	teaspoon black pepper
	Cooking oil

Wash the chicken thoroughly, and remove the excess fat. Cover the chicken in a bowl with the quart of water. Allow it to sit in the water for 3 to 4 minutes. Mix the flour, salt, and pepper. Remove the chicken from the water, shaking off only part of the water; do not pat dry (chicken should be moist). Dredge the chicken pieces in the flour mixture. In a large, deep, heavy skillet heat enough oil to cover the chicken. Place the chicken in the hot oil, and cook uncovered. Do not crowd pieces in the oil. Turn once to cook and brown the other side. When golden brown, remove from the oil, and drain on paper towels.

MAKES 4 TO 8 SERVINGS

Louis's Favorite Tuna Casserole

Tuna casserole is not particularly southern, and it's not a dish you'll likely find on the buffet tables of the Blue Willow Inn. But it is one of Louis's favorite things to eat, and Louis is a man who loves eating! This is the recipe he likes best.

1	(6-ounce) can solid white tuna packed in water
1	(9-ounce) package cooked and drained seashell noodles
1	(10 ¾-ounce) can condensed cream of mushroom soup
½	cup plus ½ cup grated Cheddar cheese
½	teaspoon salt
25	Ritz crackers, crumbled into crumbs

Preheat the oven to 350°F. Mix together the tuna, noodles, soup, ½ cup cheese, and salt. Pour the mixture into a casserole, and bake for 30 minutes. Top with the cracker crumbs and the remaining ½ cup cheese. Return the casserole to the oven only long enough for the cheese topping to melt.

MAKES 4 TO 6 SERVINGS

DESSERTS

Apple Brown Betty

We're not exactly sure what the formal difference is between a cobbler and a Betty, except in this apple Betty the crusty starch is crumbled Graham crackers and the sweetness is a sultry one, created by a mixture of molasses and brown sugar. This should be served warm with a glob of vanilla ice cream melting fast on top.

¾   plus ¾ cup graham cracker crumbs
6   peeled, cored, and sliced tart baking apples
½   cup water
½   cup molasses
¼   cup brown sugar
½   cup melted butter
½   teaspoon cinnamon

Preheat the oven to 350°F. Sprinkle ¾ cup of the graham cracker crumbs onto the bottom of a baking dish. Place half the sliced apples on top of the crumbs; repeat with the remaining ¾ cup crumbs, then the remaining half of the apples. In a bowl mix the water, molasses, sugar, and butter. Add the cinnamon. Pour this mixture evenly over the top of the apples and graham cracker crumbs. Cover and bake for 40 minutes. Uncover and bake for 15 minutes more.

MAKES 8 SERVINGS

GONE WITH THE WIND AND THE BLUE WILLOW INN

First-time visitors to the Blue Willow Inn gaze upon the mansion's majestic front porch with Corinthian columns and are reminded of another grand southern home: *Gone With the Wind's* Tara. Perhaps the best-known fictional dwelling of all time and one of the few houses to be a main character in any book, Tara may well have been inspired by the Blue Willow Inn.

After John and Bertha Upshaw built their home in 1917 to evoke an antebellum southern mansion, one of their frequent visitors was a little-known *Atlanta Journal* reporter named Margaret Mitchell, who stayed in a small Victorian cottage to the south of the main house. During the time when she used the guest house, Miss Mitchell was dating John Upshaw's cousin, a handsome bachelor named Redd Upshaw from the nearby town of Between, Georgia.

MARGARET AT THE TYPEWRITER *(COURTESY OF THE ATLANTA HISTORICAL SOCIETY)*

After a passionate courtship, he and Margaret were married, but theirs was a short and tumultous union, ending in divorce. The main problem seems to have been that Redd was a cad, not meant for a life of happy monogamy. It is generally agreed that Redd's wayward ways were the inspiration for the character of Rhett Butler in Miss Mitchell's 1936 best-selling novel, *Gone With the Wind*. There is no telling whether or not Redd Upshaw gave a damn about the Upshaw home, but there is little doubt that the pillared mansion that was the pride of Social Circle helped the author define the grandeur of Scarlett O'Hara's beloved Tara.

Banana Pudding

There are, sad to say, many parts of America where pudding is a nearly forgotten dessert. But where cooking tradition is more valued than cooking trends, pudding remains a necessary sweet. Banana pudding is especially favored in the South, where it is always made with vanilla wafers and served either swirled with meringue or crowned with whipped topping, as in this Blue Willow recipe.

6	tablespoons flour
8	tablespoons sugar
	Dash of salt
2	eggs, beaten
4	cups milk
	Vanilla wafer cookies
4	to 5 bananas, sliced
1	(9-ounce) container refrigerated whipped topping

In a saucepan combine the flour, sugar, salt, and eggs. Add the milk a little at a time, stirring until smooth. Cook over medium heat, stirring continuously until thickened. Cool thoroughly. Line the bottom of a casserole dish with the vanilla wafers then the bananas then the custard. Repeat until the dish is about ⅔ full, ending with custard. Top with the whipped topping. Refrigerate any leftovers.

MAKES 8 TO 10 SERVINGS

Blue Willow Squares

Like so much American cooking, the Blue Willow Inn's specialties include dishes that are made from scratch as well as many that use canned or boxed goods in a mix-and-match fashion. These Blue Willow Squares, a variation on what many home cooks know as Park Avenue Squares, start with an off-the-shelf cake mix but become something totally different, so dreamy-moist that you'll need a plate and fork to eat one.

1	(18-¼-ounce) package yellow cake mix
¼	pound (1 stick) butter or margarine, softened
1	cup chopped pecans
2	plus 2 eggs
1	(8-ounce) block cream cheese, softened
1	(16-ounce) package confectioners' sugar

Preheat the oven to 350°F. In a bowl mix well the cake mix, butter, pecans, and two of the eggs with a spoon. Chill your hands with ice water, and press the mixture into an 8 x 11-inch baking pan. Slightly beat the remaining two eggs, and in a separate bowl combine them with the softened cream cheese. Add the powdered sugar, and lightly mix. This mixture should be slightly lumpy. Spoon it over the cake mixture, and use the back of a spoon or spatula to spread it evenly. Bake for 45 to 50 minutes, or until dark golden brown. Cool thoroughly, at least 1 hour, and cut into squares.

MAKES 20 (2-INCH) SQUARES

Blueberry Banana Pecan Nut Cake

This wonderful cake, which has some of just about everything good in a dessert, is a frequent item on the buffet table at the Blue Willow Inn. The Van Dykes recommend it for brunch, but it's hard to imagine any meal where it wouldn't be welcome.

1	cup fresh blueberries
4	ounces (1 stick) butter, softened
1½	cups sugar
4	eggs
3	large ripe bananas, mashed
2	cups sour cream
2	cups all-purpose flour
1	teaspoon baking soda
1	teaspoon baking powder
¼	teaspoon salt
1	cup chopped pecans

Grease and flour two 9 x 5 x 2-inch loaf pans. Preheat the oven to 375°F. Rinse and drain the blueberries. In a large bowl cream the butter and sugar. Add the eggs, one at a time, mixing well. Add the bananas and sour cream, and mix well. Add the flour, baking soda, baking powder, and salt. Fold the blueberries and pecans into the batter. Pour the batter into the prepared loaf pans. Bake for 45 to 55 minutes, or until a toothpick inserted in the center comes out clean. Cool and serve.

[Serving suggestion: Top with fresh blueberries or warm Blueberry Sauce (p. 148).]

MAKES 2 LOAVES

Blueberry Cobbler

Cobblers are a popular dessert in restaurants that offer serve-yourself buffets. Unlike a pie, which starts beautiful but can get disheveled after many people have cut slices for themselves, a cobbler looks motley right from the beginning. Cobblers are always served warm. Top with a scoop of ice cream or pour on a bit of heavy cream as a garnish.

1	cup self-rising flour
1	cup sugar
1	cup milk
1	stick butter or margarine, melted
2	cups blueberries, fresh or frozen

Preheat the oven to 375°F. In a large bowl mix together the flour, sugar, milk, and butter. Place the blueberries in a baking dish. Pour the mixture over the blueberries. Bake for 35 minutes.

MAKES 8 SERVINGS

Blueberry Dessert

Although devised by the Hard Labor Creek Blueberry Farm of Social Circle, this layered sweet, known simply as blueberry dessert, will be a familiar kind of recipe to home cooks all around the country. You'll want to use the freshest, sweetest berries you can get (preferably just picked); but you also must use Cool Whip. Don't even think of substituting whipped cream for the white stuff in a tub. The amalgamation of the cream cheese/Cool Whip layer with the nutty/sweet foundation and popping fresh berries on top is an only-in-America harmony. In some parts of the country, they'd call this dessert a torte.

1	cup all-purpose flour
1	stick butter, softened
¼	cup dark brown sugar
1	cup chopped pecans
1	(8-ounce) package cream cheese, softened
1	(8-ounce) container refrigerated whipped topping
¾	plus ¼ cup sugar
1	teaspoon vanilla extract
1	quart blueberries, washed
2	heaping teaspoons cornstarch

Preheat the oven to 350°F. Combine the flour, butter, dark brown sugar, and pecans. Mix well. Press into the bottom of a 9 x 13 x 2-inch baking dish. Bake for 15 to 20 minutes until slightly brown. Remove from the oven, and cool. In another bowl mix together the cream cheese, whipped topping, ¾ cup sugar, and vanilla extract. Spread this over the cooled base, and place in the refrigerator while you cook the blueberries.

In a saucepan combine the blueberries, cornstarch, the remaining ¼ cup sugar, and just barely enough water to moisten everything. Over medium heat cook and stir until thick. Remove from the heat and cool. Spread over the cream cheese layer. Refrigerate until served.

MAKES 8 TO 10 SERVINGS

Blueberry Sauce

The main reason for making this sauce is to have it as a topping for Blueberry Banana Pecan Nut Cake (p. 145); but it also happens to be a fine substitute for syrup on morning pancakes.

¾   *cup sugar*
2   *cups water*
¼   *cup cornstarch*
24   *ounces blueberries*

Combine the sugar and water in a saucepan, and bring it to a boil. In a small bowl combine the cornstarch with a small amount of water, just enough to dissolve it. Stir the cornstarch into the boiling mixture. Add the blueberries, and lower the heat. Cook, stirring until the mixture becomes a thick syrup, and let cool thoroughly.

MAKES 1 QUART

Bourbon Sauce

By law, the staff of the Blue Willow Inn cannot even uncork a bottle of wine for a customer; and that's fine with the Van Dykes. As a matter of principle, no liquor is served at the Blue Willow Inn; but when you make bread pudding, it would be a sin to serve it without bourbon sauce.

1	stick butter
1	cup sugar
1	egg, well beaten
¼	cup bourbon

Heat the butter and sugar in the microwave oven until the sugar is dissolved. Let this mixture cool slightly. Gradually add the beaten egg, whisking vigorously so the egg does not cook. Add the bourbon, and mix. Cool and serve.

MAKES ABOUT 3 CUPS

THE ANTEBELLUM GIRLS

In the New South, one does not see too many belles sashaying around in hoop skirts and carrying parasols to protect their fair skin from the sun. But on the front porch and in the gardens of the Blue Willow Inn, they are an everyday sight throughout the spring and summer. In this setting it's hardly a shock to see them; for here the clock has stopped. This is the Old South, where beautiful wasp-waisted girls flutter about in silk gowns offering sweet tea to those who are sitting on the porch awaiting supper.

It is the job of the Antebellum Girls to make visitors welcome. They smile and chat and really do help newcomers feel comfortable in one of the rocking chairs, and they explain that sweet tea is known hereabouts as "the Champagne of the South."

If you return regularly to the Blue Willow Inn, you'll meet new Antebellum Girls each year. They are from the local school; and when they graduate, they

move on. We are quite sure that they spend most of their days in jeans and sneakers just like teenage girls everywhere. But when you see them dressed in the elaborate ensembles of long ago, their hair piled romantically atop their heads, cameos on ribbons around their slender necks, it is easy to understand why there was once a time when men fought duels for their hands and laid coats across mud puddles so they needn't soil their dainty feet.

Bread Pudding

Any time you have leftover buttermilk biscuits, this is a great dish to make. It's good with bread, too, but the biscuits give it a truly southern flavor.

4	eggs
1¾	cup sugar
½	teaspoon vanilla extract
¼	teaspoon cinnamon
¼	teaspoon nutmeg
1	stick butter, softened
4	cups milk
8	to 10 leftover biscuits or ½ loaf toasted white bread
¾	cup raisins

Preheat the oven to 350°F. In a large mixing bowl beat the eggs until frothy. Add the sugar, vanilla, cinnamon, and nutmeg. Beat well. Add the butter and milk. Beat well. Coarsely crumble the biscuits or bread, and add to the mixture. Add the raisins. Mix well, but do not beat. Pour into an ungreased 13 x 9 x 2-inch pan. Bake for 40 to 45 minutes, or until brown. Serve warm with Lemon Sauce (p.178).

MAKES 8 TO 10 SERVINGS

Buttermilk Pie

Deluxe desserts are fine, but some of the best country classics are edible simplicity. Buttermilk pie is as basic as can be, and while it is possible for one's head to be turned at the buffet table by more elaborate confections, it would be a grievous error to neglect this perfect pastry.

3	*eggs, slightly beaten*
1	*cup sugar*
2	*tablespoons flour*
½	*cup melted butter*
1	*cup buttermilk*
½	*teaspoon vanilla*
½	*teaspoon lemon extract*
1	*unbaked (9-inch) pastry pie shell*

Preheat the oven to 350°F. Combine the eggs, sugar, flour, and butter in a bowl, and mix well. Add the buttermilk, vanilla, and lemon extract, and mix. Pour into the pie shell. Bake for 45 to 50 minutes, or until the pie is set and golden brown.

MAKES 8 SERVINGS

Chewy Oatmeal Cookies

The pies and cakes on the dessert table in the buffet room are so alluring that it is easy to overlook cookies set out for the taking. After three or four return trips for more forkworthy desserts, who can even think about cookies? At home, where we generally face one dessert at a time, it's easy to pay more attention to the simpler things in life, like these classic chewy cookies from the Blue Willow collection.

¾	cup butter-flavored shortening
1¼	cups firmly packed light brown sugar
1	egg
⅓	cup milk
1½	teaspoons vanilla extract
3	cups Quaker Oats, quick or old-fashioned, uncooked
1	cup all-purpose flour
½	teaspoon baking soda
½	teaspoon salt
¼	teaspoon cinnamon
1	cup raisins
1	cup coarsely chopped walnuts

Preheat the oven to 375°F. Lightly grease a baking sheet with a small amount of shortening. In a large mixing bowl combine the shortening with the brown sugar, egg, milk, and vanilla. Beat at medium speed until well blended. Combine the oats, flour, baking soda, salt, and cinnamon. Mix into the creamed mixture at low speed until blended. Stir in the raisins and nuts. Drop rounded tablespoons of dough 2 inches apart on the prepared baking sheet. Bake for 10 to 12 minutes, or until light brown.

MAKES ABOUT 30 COOKIES

Melanie's Chocolate Chip Cookies

Plump and buttery, these fragile cookies are a legacy of the mother of former Blue Willow employee Melanie Jackson. Melanie's mom hailed from Missouri, but chocolate chip cookies such as these are a favorite pretty much everywhere in the U.S.A.

1¾	cups all-purpose flour
1	teaspoon baking soda
1	teaspoon salt
2	eggs
2	sticks butter, melted and cooled
¾	cup firmly packed light brown sugar
¼	cup sugar
1	(3.4-ounce) package instant vanilla pudding
1	teaspoon vanilla
1	(12-ounce) package semi-sweet chocolate chips

In a bowl combine the flour, baking soda, and salt. In a separate bowl combine the eggs and butter. Mix with an electric mixer until creamy. Add the brown and white sugars, pudding, and vanilla, and mix well. Slowly add the flour mixture. After all is well mixed, fold in the chocolate chips. Preheat the oven to 375°F. Drop the batter by heaping teaspoonfuls, two inches apart, onto a prepared cookie sheet. Bake for 11 to 13 minutes on the center rack of the oven until cookies are tan. Use a spatula to carefully remove the warm cookies from the cookie sheet, and place them on a wire rack to cool.

MAKES ABOUT 36 (2 TO 2½-INCH) COOKIES

Chess Pie

"Whether you like vinegar or cornmeal, this is a must-try pie," the Van Dykes say. "You would never know the ingredients unless you made the pie." Like the famous mock apple pie made from soda crackers, chess pie truly is an oven miracle that uses bare-cupboard ingredients but winds up tasting opulent. Food historians speculate on its name; and the best explanation we've found is that long ago a happy eater asked the cook what the heck was in this delicious pie that contained no recognizable fruits or flavored fillings, but had such a satisfying character. The cook thought a while and said that there was virtually nothing in it, that it was "Just pie." Just pie sounded like jes' pie which eventually became chess pie, now a staple among southern pastry chefs.

2	cups sugar
1	tablespoon all-purpose flour
2	tablespoons yellow cornmeal
½	cup butter, melted
1	tablespoon white vinegar
½	teaspoons vanilla extract
4	eggs
¼	cup buttermilk
¼	teaspoon salt
1	(9-inch) piecrust, unbaked

Preheat the oven to 350°F. In a large bowl combine the sugar, flour, cornmeal, butter, vinegar, vanilla, eggs, buttermilk, and salt. Pour the mixture into the crust. Bake for 50 minutes. Cool on a wire rack before serving.

MAKES 8 SERVINGS

Chocolate Cookie Sheet Cake

One of the best sweet things on the dessert table is a moist chocolate cake topped with chocolate icing, made from a recipe given to the Van Dykes by Pat Whitley from the nearby town of Monroe. Like so many of America's kitchens, the Blue Willow Inn uses a wide range of recipes gathered from neighbors, friends, and family.

2	cups flour
2	cups sugar
½	teaspoon salt
3	tablespoons cocoa
2	sticks margarine, melted
1	cup water
2	eggs, well beaten
1	teaspoon baking soda
½	cup buttermilk
1	teaspoon vanilla extract

Preheat the oven to 350°F. In a bowl sift the flour with the sugar and salt. Combine the cocoa, margarine, and water in a saucepan. Bring it to a boil, and pour it over the flour and sugar mixture. In a separate bowl combine the beaten eggs, baking soda, buttermilk, and vanilla. Beat well. Add to the first mixture, and mix well. Bake in a greased and floured shallow pan for 20 minutes.

While this is cooking, make the Chocolate Cookie Sheet Cake Icing (p. 157).

Chocolate Cookie Sheet Cake Icing

This is the required icing for Chocolate Cookie Sheet Cake. Make it when the cake has been in the oven for about 10 or 15 minutes so it is ready to pour over the cake as soon as the cake is ready.

2	sticks butter, melted
6	tablespoons cocoa
1	scant cup milk
2	(16-ounce) packages confectioners' sugar
2	cups chopped pecans
2	tablespoons vanilla extract

Mix the butter, cocoa, and milk in a saucepan. Heat over low heat, but do not boil. Remove from the heat and gradually add the sugar, pecans, and vanilla extract. Pour the icing over the hot cake as soon as the cake is removed from the oven.

MAKES ONE LARGE SHEET CAKE

Chocolate Macaroons

Nancy East, long-time hostess at the Blue Willow Inn, got this recipe at a U.S. Marine Corps wives' coffee in Norfolk, Virginia, in 1965. "Not only do the customers love Nancy," the Van Dykes wrote, "but she loves the customers. She is the epitome of southern hospitality."

4	egg whites
1	cup sugar
½	teaspoon salt
2	teaspoons vanilla extract
12	ounces semisweet chocolate bits
2⅔	cups shredded coconut

In a bowl beat the egg whites until stiff. Slowly add the sugar, salt, and vanilla while continuing to beat. Preheat the oven to 350°F. Melt the chocolate bits. Fold the chocolate and coconut into the egg white mixture. Drop by rounded teaspoonfuls onto lightly greased cookie sheets. Bake for 10 to 15 minutes.

MAKES ABOUT 4 DOZEN

Chocolate Meringue Pie

Like all meringue pies, this one must be watched vigilantly for its short stay in the oven. There's nothing nicer than wispy, golden-brown edges on a swirled-high meringue . . . but no one likes it burnt.

1	cup sugar
3	heaping tablespoons all-purpose flour
3	heaping tablespoons cocoa
3	large eggs, separated (reserve whites at room temperature for making meringue)
1½	cups milk
1	teaspoon vanilla extract
1	(9-inch) pie shell, baked
⅓	cup powdered sugar
½	teaspoon cream of tartar

In a saucepan combine the sugar, flour, and cocoa. Stir to remove any lumps in the cocoa. In a bowl beat the egg yolks, and add to the dry ingredients. Gradually stir in the milk. Place over medium heat, stirring constantly so that the mixture does not burn. Cook until it thickens. Remove the mixture from the heat, add the vanilla, and stir well. Pour the mixture into the baked pie shell.

Preheat the oven to 475°F. Make the meringue by beating the powdered sugar with the egg whites and cream of tartar until light and fluffy, about 3 to 4 minutes. Spread over the pie, making sure the meringue touches the crust all around. Bake the pie for 5 minutes until the meringue is golden brown. Refrigerate the pie before serving.

MAKES 8 SERVINGS

Crème De Menthe Squares

Sandi McClain, the Blue Willow Inn Gift Shop manager, cooks these wonderful mint squares during the holidays for the employees and staff of the Blue Willow Inn. Always a favorite, the staff waits in expectation each holiday for the treats.

½	plus ½ cup butter, softened
1	cup granulated sugar
2	cups confectioners' sugar
4	beaten eggs
1	cup all-purpose flour
½	teaspoon salt
1	(16-ounce) can chocolate syrup
1	teaspoon vanilla
2	tablespoons green crème de menthe syrup
1	cup chocolate chips, melted
6	tablespoons butter, melted

For the first layer, preheat the oven to 350°F. In a medium bowl cream ½ cup butter with the granulated sugar. Add the eggs, and mix. Add the flour, salt, chocolate syrup, and vanilla, and blend well. Pour the mixture into a greased 13 x 9-inch pan. Bake for 20 to 25 minutes, and let cool.

For the second layer, in a medium bowl combine the confectioners' sugar, the remaining ½ cup softened butter, and the crème de menthe. Spread the mixture over the first layer.

For the third layer, in a medium bowl combine the chocolate chips and the melted butter. Let the chocolate mixture cool, and spread it on top of the layers. Allow them to cool long enough to become firm before cutting into squares.

MAKES 18 TO 20 SQUARES

Chocolate Cherry Cake

The staff members of the Blue Willow Inn do not come to work, punch a time clock, put in their hours, then go home. They are more like a large extended family; and if you are lucky enough to poke around in the kitchen while meal-prep is in progress, you will feel like you are in the midst of a huge holiday meal being made by a slew of aunts, uncles, cousins, and relations near and far. It's noisy, confusing, funny, sometimes argumentative; spirits always run high. Given that sense of camaraderie, it's no surprise that when one of the staff members has something to celebrate or a sorrow to share, that person never feels alone. For the happy occasions, Nellie Baines, one of Blue Willow's managers, frequently makes this sumptuously sweet cake for employees only.

1	can cherry pie filling
1	(18 ¼-ounce) package fudge cake mix
1	teaspoon plus 1 tablespoon almond extract
2	eggs, beaten
1	cup sugar
5	tablespoons butter
½	cup milk
1	(6-ounce) package semisweet chocolate chips

Grease and flour a 9 x 13-inch baking pan or casserole dish. Preheat the oven to 350°F. Drain the liquid from the cherry pie filling into a mixing bowl, and set the cherries aside. Add the cake mix, 1 teaspoon almond extract, and eggs to the drained liquid. Mix well. Fold in the cherries. Pour into the prepared baking pan. Bake for 30 to 35 minutes, or until cake tests done. Remove from the oven, and cool.

To prepare the frosting: in a small saucepan combine the sugar, butter, and milk. Bring to a boil, and boil for 1 minute, stirring constantly. Remove from the heat, and add the 1 tablespoon almond extract and the chocolate chips. Beat with a mixer until smooth. Allow to cool, and spread over the cake.

MAKES 16 TO 20 SERVINGS

Coca-Cola Cake with Broiled Peanut Butter Frosting

The Van Dykes have borrowed one of our own favorite dessert recipes, which we published ten years earlier in a cookbook called Square Meals. We hope you will pardon our ego if we tell you that this cake is moist and delicious and is gobbled up with glee even by the fussiest gourmets we know! (It's okay to substitute Pepsi for Coke, but under no circumstances should diet versions of either beverage be used.)

Cake:		Frosting:	
2	cups flour	6	tablespoons butter
2	cups sugar	1	cup dark brown sugar
2	sticks butter, melted	⅔	cup creamy peanut butter
2	tablespoons unsweetened cocoa	¼	cup milk
1	cup Coca-Cola (with fizz)	⅔	cup chopped peanuts
½	cup buttermilk		
2	eggs, beaten		
1	teaspoon baking soda		
1	teaspoon vanilla extract		
1 ½	cups miniature marshmallows		

To make the cake: preheat the oven to 350°F. Grease and flour a 9 x 13 x 2-inch sheet cake pan. Combine the flour and sugar in large bowl. In a separate bowl combine the melted butter, cocoa, and Coke, and pour over the flour and sugar mixture. Stir until well blended. Add the buttermilk, eggs, baking soda, and vanilla. Mix well. Stir in the marshmallows. Pour into the prepared pan, and bake for 40 minutes. Remove the cake from the oven, and frost while still barely warm.

To make the frosting: in a bowl cream the butter, sugar, and peanut butter. Beat in the milk. Fold in the peanuts. Spread over the cake. Place the frosted cake under the broiler about 4 inches from the heat source. Broil just a few seconds, or until topping starts to bubble. **Watch constantly, being careful not to scorch** the frosting. Let cool at least 30 minutes before serving.

MAKES 1 LARGE SHEET CAKE

Coconut Cream Pie

Coconut cream pie is all-American, but it is especially popular in the South, where it is almost guaranteed to be a featured attraction at any decent small-town lunch counter, neighborhood cafeteria, or country kitchen.

Meringue:

3	egg whites
¼	teaspoon cream of tarter
6	tablespoons confectioners' sugar
½	teaspoon vanilla

Filling:

½	cup sugar
2	tablespoons corn starch
½	teaspoon salt
2	cups milk
3	egg yolks, slightly beaten
1	tablespoon soften butter
1	teaspoon vanilla
1	cup flaked coconut
1	(8-inch) precooked pie shell

To make the meringue, with an electric mixer beat the egg whites and cream of tarter until foamy. Beat in the sugar 1 tablespoon at a time. Continue beating until glossy, stiff peaks form. Fold in the vanilla.

To make the filling, combine the sugar, cornstarch, and salt into the top of a double boiler. In a bowl mix together the milk and egg yolks and gradually stir into the sugar mixture. Cook over medium heat, stirring constantly until the mixture thickens and boils. Boil for 1 minute, stirring constantly. Remove from the heat and mix in the butter and vanilla. Fold in ¾ cup of the coconut. Pour the mixture into the pie shell immediately.

Preheat the oven to 350°F. Heap the meringue over the filling, spreading it to the edge of the pie shell to prevent shrinking or weeping. Sprinkle the remaining coconut on top. Bake the pie until the meringue is golden brown, about 12 minutes.

MAKES 8 SERVINGS

Dirt Cake

Who said that cooking has to be difficult? Who said that cake making requires any baking whatsoever? The Blue Willow Inn's Dirt Cake may shock epicures by its complete lack of culinary activity (just put a few things together), but it will be familiar to back-of-the-box gourmets all across America. And when it's set out on the buffet table, it disappears just as fast, if not faster, than desserts that actually require cooking skill!

---

2   (12-ounce) packages refrigerated whipped topping

1   large (20-ounce) package Oreo cookies, all but 10 broken into crumbs

1   (16-ounce) can cherry pie filling

Cover the bottom of a clear glass bowl with refrigerated whipped topping. Add about ⅓ of the Oreo cookie crumbs, spreading them evenly over the topping. Add the cherry pie filling. Add another layer of topping and a layer of cookie crumbs. Add one more layer of topping and the last of the cookie crumbs. Top with whole Oreos. Refrigerate 2 to 3 hours to allow flavors to harmonize, and serve chilled.

MAKES 8 SERVINGS

Fresh Apple Cake

A Social Circle recipe contributed to the inn by retired manager and friend Elton Wright, this cake is a good make-ahead snack, especially well suited for afternoon tea or coffee.

2	*cups sugar*
½	*cup vegetable oil*
3	*eggs*
3	*cups all-purpose flour*
1	*teaspoon salt*
1	*teaspoon baking soda*
1½	*teaspoons vanilla extract*
3	*cups peeled and diced firm Granny Smith apples*
¾	*cup flaked coconut*
1	*cup pecan pieces*

Oil and lightly flour a 9-inch pound cake pan or tube pan. Preheat the oven to 325°F. In a large bowl mix together the sugar and oil. Add the eggs, and beat well. Combine the flour, salt, and baking soda, and add to the oil mixture. Stir in the vanilla, apples, coconut, and nuts. Spoon the mixture into the prepared pan. Bake for 80 to 90 minutes. Cool and serve.

MAKES 1 POUND CAKE

MANNERS CLASS

Throughout the school year, groups of children from nearby grade schools are bussed to the Blue Willow Inn at lunchtime for a meal and a manners lesson. On November 15, 2001, one such class of fifty-five third graders came from the Social Circle Elementary School. The students gathered in a semicircle around the front steps of the inn as Billie Van Dyke stood on the porch and announced, "Good morning, everybody!"

This was a group of well-prepared boys and girls, already on their way to a life of good behavior. Some boys wore jackets and ties; girls wore pretty dresses and ribbons in their hair. In unison, they all responded, "Good morning!"

"Welcome to the Blue Willow Inn," Billie added, then got right to the business at hand. "When you go into a restaurant, do you run in screaming?"

"No!" the children shouted.

Reading from a well-worn code of etiquette that she has used many times for many groups of children, Billie continued the lesson. "The gentleman tells the host how many are in your party. Boys should always wait until the girls or ladies are seated, and should pull their chairs out and push them back in gently."

The children filed up onto the porch, past the grand Corinthian columns, and into the Lewis Grizzard Room, where they took seats. Some boys apparently already knew how to help seat a girl; but a few gave their chair a vigorously playful shove. Some of the smaller boys faced the daunting task of pushing in the chairs of girls much larger than themselves.

Once everyone was seated, Billie stood at one end of the room and resumed the lesson. "When you talk, do you holler and scream across the room to your friends at other tables?"

"No!" the children screamed in happy unanimity.

"Because we are the Blue Willow Inn and we serve our food buffet style, you will find our plates on the table in front of you. You can see the Blue Willow pattern on them," Billie explained with pride. "Now, take your napkin and put it across your lap. And when you stand up to go to the buffet line, put it on the left-hand side of where the plate has been." Next came a tough question: "Who can tell me why you have two forks?"

A small boy dressed in a blue blazer with a tie and pressed shirt timidly raised his hand. "For salad and dinner?" he ventured in a voice not yet changed.

"That's right!" Billie beamed. "And what about the spoon and fork above your plate?

No one could field that one.

"They are for dessert," Billie revealed. "Does anybody know the proper way to hold knife and fork?"

At this question the children picked up their utensils in all sorts of ways, some with practiced elegance, others in a mischievous imitation of a lout clutching a hammer.

"Do you cut large pieces?" Billie asked.

"No!" the children agreed.

"That's right. You cut them bite sized. And the rule is that you cut only three pieces of meat at one time."

The education continued: "Do we blow bubbles with our straws?"

Again, a chorused "No!"

"It's a temptation, though, isn't it?" Billie replied with genuine empathy..

After discussion about the proper way to eat soup (dipping the spoon away from you and never slurping), came the final question. "How do you tell the waitress you are finished?" Nobody knew.

"You rest your knife with the cutting blade toward the inside of the plate. Some people say at three o'clock, others say at four o'clock. Once your silverware is at rest, you sit quietly with your hands in your lap and your feet on the floor . . . if they reach the floor."

Finally, before sending them off to get their lunch, Billie noted, "What's good about a buffet is that you can try things you're not familiar with." However, few of the boys and girls selected the Blue Willow's gloriously tender liver and onions or even the lusciously cheesy broccoli casserole. They stuck with fried chicken, biscuits, and mashed potatoes. Because it was "manners day" for youngsters, the buffet offered one food found at no other time on the Blue Willow's tables: franks and beans.

Fried Pie

Here is a dessert that combines the sweetness of pie and the lusciousness of fried food. Individual-serving fried pies are a dessert that is favored throughout the South; and although the Blue Willow's version is filled with Georgia's favorite fruit, peaches, a fried pie is good with apples, berries, and cherries, too. This is an especially easy recipe, because it does not demand you make the pastry dough from scratch. Simply roll out some canned biscuits from the refrigerator case at the grocery store.

1   *(12-ounce) bag dried peaches*

1   *cup sugar*

2   *cups water*

6   *canned biscuits, uncooked*

1   *cup flour*

2   *cups cooking oil*

In a large saucepan, combine the peaches, sugar, and water. Cook on low heat until the peaches are tender. Drain the peaches. On a lightly floured surface, roll out each biscuit into a thin sheet. Fill each sheet on one side with the peaches. Fold the other side over, and seal it with a fork. Dredge the pies in the flour. Heat the oil in a large skillet, and cook the pies on each side until brown, turning twice. Drain on paper bags.

For fried pies with apple filling, substitute dried apples for the peaches. Follow the same directions, but add ½ teaspoon of cinnamon and ½ teaspoon of apple pie spice.

[Note: When drained on paper towels, the pies have a tendency to stick to the towels.]

MAKES 6 PIES

Frozen Lemon Squares

A ribboned festival of luxurious ingredients shot through with the zest of lemon. These squares are best served 10 to 15 minutes out of the freezer so they are still icy cold but blossoming with flavor as they begin to thaw.

¼	cup butter or margarine
1¼	cups graham cracker crumbs
¼	cup sugar
3	egg yolks
1	(14-ounce) can sweetened condensed milk
½	cup lemon juice from concentrate
	Refrigerated whipped topping, thawed
	Lemon peel for garnish

In a large bowl combine the butter, graham cracker crumbs, and sugar. Press the mixture into the bottom of an 8 or 9-inch square pan. In a medium bowl beat the egg yolks. Stir in the sweetened condensed milk and the lemon juice. Pour into the prepared crust. Top with the whipped topping. Freeze the pie for 4 to 6 hours, or until firm. Let it stand for 10 minutes before cutting. Garnish with lemon peel.

MAKES 6 TO 8 SERVINGS

Fresh Coconut Cake from Scratch

Billie and Louis Van Dyke have proclaimed this "the best cake ever." We who are coconut cake lovers must agree. Not only is it moist, fluffy, and sweet; it is utterly beautiful—a tall, layered classic. Topped with 7-minute icing and generously sprinkled with tender shreds of coconut, it is suitable for Sunday supper, holiday meals, birthdays, and wedding anniversaries.

1	cup butter
2	cups sugar
4	eggs
3	cups all-purpose flour
2	teaspoons baking powder
¼	teaspoon baking soda
¼	teaspoon salt
1	cup milk
1	teaspoon vanilla
½	teaspoon lemon juice

Preheat the oven to 350°F. Cream the butter and sugar. Add the beaten eggs (egg whites are optional). Sift together the flour, baking power, baking soda, and salt. Add the flour mixture to the butter/sugar/egg mixture alternately with the milk (at the Blue Willow Inn, we start with flour and end with flour). Makes three (thicker) 9-inch layers or four (thinner) 9-inch layers. Bake the cake for 20 to 25 minutes, or until a toothpick inserted into the center comes out clean. While the cake is baking, make the 7-Minute Icing (p. 171).

7-Minute Icing

3 egg whites
1 ⅔ cups sugar
¼ cup white corn syrup
¼ cup coconut milk (or water)
    Dash of salt
1 teaspoon vanilla or lemon juice
    (either ingredient accomplishes the desired flavor)
3 to 4 cups freshly grated coconut

Cook the egg whites, sugar, corn syrup, coconut milk, and salt in a double boiler for 7 minutes, beating with a hand mixer until peaks begin to drop off spoon. Remove from the heat, and add the vanilla. Spread the icing between the layers and on the sides—and don't to forget to sprinkle freshly grated coconut all over as you go.

This beautiful masterpiece can be dressed up for any holiday occasion—birthdays, wedding anniversaries, church socials, and Sunday suppers.

MAKES 1 CAKE

Julian's Pecan Pie

Julian is Louis Van Dyke's father, who bakes pecan pie for friends and neighbors every year at Thanksgiving and Christmas. You can count on pecan pie every day at the Blue Willow buffet tables; it is a staple of kitchens throughout the South. Julian's version is more sophisticated than most, in that the corn syrup is balanced by pure maple.

3	eggs, slightly beaten
½	cup dark corn syrup
½	cup pure maple syrup
½	cup sugar
2½	tablespoons margarine, melted
1	teaspoon vanilla extract
1	teaspoon pure lemon extract
1	cup pecans
1	frozen pastry piecrust, thawed

Preheat the oven to 350°F. In a large bowl combine the eggs, corn and maple syrups, sugar, margarine, and vanilla and lemon extracts, and stir until well-blended. Add the pecans, and stir enough to spread them evenly. Pour into the thawed piecrust, and bake for 50 to 55 minutes. When the pie is cooled, it can be garnished with whipped cream or whipped topping. Or it can be served warm with vanilla ice cream.

MAKES 8 SERVINGS

Julian's Sweet Potato Pie

Although throughout the year, sweet potato pie appears regularly on the dessert menus of plate-lunch restaurants and barbecue shacks, as the autumn harvest approaches, sweet potatoes are even more on people's minds. The Van Dykes write that this pie is "a must with Thanksgiving and Christmas dinners." Their recipe for the southern classic comes from Louis's father, Julian.

2	cups cooked, mashed sweet potatoes
1	cup sugar
¼	cup butter or margarine, melted
¼	teaspoon salt
1	teaspoon vanilla extract
1	teaspoon pure lemon extract
1	(14-ounce) can sweetened condensed milk
2	eggs, slightly beaten
1	teaspoon ground cinnamon
½	teaspoon ground ginger
1	teaspoon ground nutmeg
1	(9-inch) frozen, flaky piecrust
	Whipped cream, optional

Preheat the oven to 425°F. In a large bowl combine the potatoes, sugar, butter, salt, vanilla and lemon extracts, condensed milk, eggs, cinnamon, ginger, and nutmeg, and mix well. Pour into the frozen piecrust. Bake for 15 minutes. Reduce the heat to 350°F, and bake for 35 to 40 minutes more. If desired, garnish each slice with a small amount of whipped cream and nutmeg.

MAKES 8 SERVINGS

Key Lime Pie

Fresh lime juice is essential for a full-flavored pie. If you can secure real Key limes or their juice from Florida, they're much better. A real Key lime pie is as yellow as lemons (that's a Key lime's color) but has a mellow flavor all its own.

1	(14-ounce) can sweetened condensed milk
½	cup fresh lime juice
3	large egg yolks, lightly beaten
1	(9-inch) pie shell, cooked
3	large egg whites
¼	teaspoon cream of tartar
6	tablespoons sugar

Preheat the oven to 325°F. In a bowl combine the condensed milk and lime juice. Blend in the egg yolks. Pour the mixture into the cooked pie shell. In another bowl beat the egg whites with the cream of tartar until soft peaks form. Beat the sugar into the egg whites one tablespoon at a time until the egg whites form stiff glossy peaks. Spoon the egg whites over the pie filling, and spread to the edge. Bake 15 minutes, or until golden. Cool the pie on a wire rack before serving.

MAKES 8 SERVINGS

Lemon Meringue Pie

After a meal of kaleidoscopic flavors and a substantial number of calories, few desserts feel more appropriate than lemon meringue pie. Its crisp flavor and airy meringue are a cool breeze for a weary palate.

1⅓	cups sugar
½	cup cornstarch
⅛	teaspoon salt
1¾	cups cold water
4	eggs, separated (reserve whites at room temperature for making meringue)
3	tablespoons butter
2	tablespoons grated lemon rind
¼	cup lemon juice
1	(9-inch) baked pastry pie shell
⅓	cup powdered sugar
½	teaspoon cream of tartar

Combine the sugar, cornstarch, and salt in a saucepan. Over medium heat, gradually add the water, stirring until smooth. Stir constantly. Cook until the mixture thickens and comes to a low boil. Boil 1 minute, stirring continuously. Remove from the heat, and let cool until tepid. In a large bowl beat the egg yolks at high speed until thick. Gradually stir about one-third of the tepid sugar mixture into the egg yolks; then add the warmed egg yolks to the remaining sugar mixture. Stir constantly as you do this. Return the pan to the heat, and cook 2 to 3 minutes longer, continuing to stir. Remove from the heat. Add the butter, lemon rind, and lemon juice, stirring to mix. Pour the warm filling into pastry pie shell.

Preheat the oven to 350°F. Make the meringue by beating the powdered sugar with the egg whites and cream of tartar until light and fluffy, about 3 to 4 minutes. Spread over the pie, making sure the meringue touches the crust all around. Bake 12 to 14 minutes until the meringue is browned. Let the pie cool before serving.

MAKES 8 SERVINGS

Lane Cake

Every southern Lady serves this wonderful cake at special occasions—a family reunion, an Easter Sunday dinner, a special guest comes for supper. All those great occasions are enjoyed around the table.

1	*cup butter or margarine, softened*
1	*cup sugar*
3¼	*cups sifted cake flour*
2	*teaspoons baking powder*
	Pinch of salt
1	*cup milk*
2	*teaspoons vanilla extract*
8	*egg whites, stiffly beaten*
	Filling and frosting (recipes follow)

Preheat the oven to 375°F. In a bowl cream the butter. Gradually add the sugar, beating with an electric mixer until light and fluffy. In another bowl combine the cake flour, baking powder, and salt; stir well. Add the flour mixture to the creamed mixture alternately with the milk, beating well after each addition. Stir in the vanilla. Fold in the egg whites. Pour the batter into three greased and floured 9-inch cake pans. Bake for 20 minutes, or until the cake tests done. Cool in the pans for 10 minutes. Remove the cakes from the pans, and let them cool completely. Spread the filling (p. 177) between the layers, and spread the top and sides of the cake with the frosting (p. 177).

Filling:

8	*large egg yolks*
1	*cup sugar*
½	*cup butter or margarine*
1	*cup golden raisins, finely chopped*
⅓	*cup bourbon or brandy*
1	*teaspoon vanilla extract*

Combine the egg yolks, sugar, and butter in a 2-quart saucepan. Cook over medium heat, stirring constantly, until thickened, about 20 minutes. Remove from the heat, and stir in the raisins, bourbon, and vanilla. Let the filling cool before spreading on the cake.

Frosting:

½	*cup sugar*
¼	*cup light corn syrup*
2	*teaspoons water*
⅛	*teaspoon salt*
2	*egg whites*
½	*teaspoon vanilla extract*

Combine the sugar, corn syrup, water, and salt in a heavy saucepan. Cook over medium heat, stirring constantly, until the mixture is clear. Continue cooking until the mixture reaches 245°F. In a bowl beat the egg whites until soft peaks form, and continue to beat the egg whites while slowly adding the syrup mixture. Add the vanilla. Continue beating until stiff peaks form and the frosting is thick enough to spread.

MAKES ONE 3-LAYER CAKE

Lemon Sauce

For bread pudding or hot gingerbread, this is the crowning touch.

1	cup water
2½	cups sugar
½	teaspoons cornstarch
⅛	teaspoon salt
2	tablespoons melted butter
1½	teaspoons lemon juice
1½	teaspoons grated lemon rind
	Dash of nutmeg

Bring the water to a boil in a saucepan, and add the sugar, cornstarch, salt, butter, lemon juice, lemon rind, and nutmeg; stir well. Continue stirring for 2 to 3 minutes until well blended. If the sauce is too thin, add a small amount of dissolved cornstarch. Remove from the heat. Cool. Serve at room temperature.

MAKES ABOUT 3 CUPS

Lots of Louis's Brownies

The Blue Willow Inn cooks in quantities that are usually way too large for average home cooks. But if there is ever a time when you need to make enough brownies for a big party, try this recipe, a favorite of Louis's. It relies on boxed brownie mix as its foundation, but the mix is doctored up to be nuttier and chewier.

2	*(19.5-ounce) packages brownie mix*
⅓	*cup chocolate icing*
1	*cup chopped pecans*
½	*cup sugar*
	Solid vegetable shortening
	Sugar for dusting pans

Preheat the oven to 350°F. Follow the directions on the brownie mix box, using one fewer egg per box and ¼ cup less vegetable oil. In a large bowl combine the ingredients listed on the box, the chocolate icing, and the chopped pecans. Mix gently, but do not beat. Grease two 9 x 13-inch sheet pans with shortening, and coat with sugar. Pour the brownie mix onto each pan, and spread evenly. Bake for 15 to 17 minutes.

[Note: Remove the brownies from the oven while the center of the pans is still slightly loose. If this recipe is cooked until the center is firm, the brownies will wind up hard and overcooked.]

MAKE AT LEAST 5 DOZEN

Mints

Mints are a must for parties and special occasions. Store-bought mints can never compare to homemade mints.

⅓   cup light corn syrup

4   tablespoons butter, softened

1   teaspoon peppermint extract

½   teaspoon salt

1   (16-ounce) package confectioners' sugar, sifted
    Food coloring

In a bowl blend the corn syrup, butter, peppermint extract, and salt. Add the sugar, and mix by hand with a spoon until smooth. Add 1 drop of food coloring for each ⅓ cup of the mixture. Press the mixture into desired mint molds. Let the molds stand for several hours to dry. Store in a sealed container.

   [Note: If mint molds are not available, roll a small amount of mixture into a nickel-sized ball, and flatten with a fork onto wax paper.]

MAKES ABOUT 7 DOZEN

1-2-3-4 Cake

Nearly as easy as A-B-C, this fundamental sugar-butter-egg pound cake was the first cake Billie Van Dyke ever baked.

1	cup (2 sticks) butter, softened
2	cups sugar
4	eggs
3	cups all-purpose flour
1	tablespoon baking powder
¼	teaspoon salt
1	cup milk
1	teaspoon vanilla

Preheat the oven to 350°F. In a bowl cream the butter and sugar until light and fluffy. Add the eggs, one at a time, beating well after each addition. In a separate bowl sift together the flour, baking powder, and salt. Add the dry ingredients to the batter alternately with the milk, beating well after each addition. Add the vanilla, and pour the batter into a greased and floured tube pan. Bake for 1 hour, or until the cake pulls away from the sides of the pan. Turn the cake out onto a cooling rack.

MAKES ONE TUBE CAKE

Orange Coconut Cake

One of the reasons we enjoy eating our way around the South is that we like coconut cake. One of the goopiest, coconutiest recipes we've ever found is this one from the Blue Willow Inn.

1	(18-¼-ounce) box Duncan Hines Orange Supreme Cake Mix
1	(3-ounce) package orange flavored gelatin
1	cup water
⅓	cup vegetable oil
2	eggs
1	plus 1 teaspoon orange flavoring
1	(16-ounce) package sour cream
¼	cup frozen orange juice
1	(12-ounce) package shredded coconut
2	cups sugar
1	(8-ounce) package refrigerated whipped topping
1	cup mandarin oranges, drained

In a large bowl combine the cake mix, gelatin, water, oil, eggs, and 1 teaspoon of the orange flavoring. Mix well, and pour into four prepared 8-inch pans. Bake according to directions on the cake mix box. Cool.

For the filling: in a bowl combine the sour cream, orange juice, coconut, sugar, and the remaining 1 teaspoon of orange flavoring. Mix well. Reserve 1 cup of the filling for the frosting. Spread the remaining filling between the layers of the cake. Fold the topping into the reserved 1 cup of filling. Spread this on the top and sides of the cake. Decorate with the mandarin oranges. Refrigerate for 6 to 8 hours.

MAKES 1 FOUR-LAYER CAKE

Peach Cobbler

No meal at the Blue Willow Inn is complete without at least a taste of peach cobbler. No matter what other desserts may be arrayed in the center of the buffet room, you can always count on a big pan of peach cobbler set out on the side where bowls of it can supplement any other end-of-meal sweet.

(Note: Fresh or canned peaches can be used. When using fresh, peel and slice them, sprinkling the slices with an additional ½ cup of sugar, and refrigerate for 2 to 3 hours before using.)

⅔   cup plus 2 tablespoons sugar

1   cup self-rising flour

¼   plus ¼ cup melted butter

1   (28-ounce) can sliced peaches

Preheat the oven to 350°F. In a bowl coarsely mix the ⅔ cup sugar, flour, and ¼ cup melted butter. Sprinkle about one-third of this mixture on the bottom of a baking dish. Add the peaches and juice. Top the peaches with the remaining flour mixture. Sprinkle the top with two tablespoons sugar and the remaining ¼ cup butter. Bake for 30 to 40 minutes, or until brown and bubbly. Serve hot.

[Note: If the juice from the peaches does not cover peaches, add a small amount of water just to cover the peaches. Too little liquid will make the cobbler dry. Too much liquid will make the cobbler soupy.]

MAKES 6 TO 8 SERVINGS

Peanut Butter Layer Cake with Peanut Butter Frosting

If you live in the same county with someone who has peanut allergies, we recommend not making this cake. On the other hand, if you like what happens to the taste of peanuts when they are sweetened and baked, here is bliss on a dish.

Cake:

½	cup solid vegetable shortening
1	cup creamy peanut butter
1½	cups sugar
3	eggs
2	cups all-purpose flour
1	teaspoon baking soda
1½	cups buttermilk
1	teaspoon vanilla extract

Frosting:

1	stick butter, softened
1	(16-ounce) package confectioners' sugar
1	cup peanut butter, creamy or chunky as desired
½	teaspoon vanilla extract
	Milk, as needed

Grease and sugar three layer-cake pans. Preheat the oven to 350°F. In a bowl cream the shortening, peanut butter, and sugar. Add the eggs one at a time, beating after each addition. In a separate bowl combine the flour with the baking soda, and add to the mixture alternately with the buttermilk, beating after each addition. Add the vanilla, and mix well. Bake for 30 minutes. Remove from the oven, and after the cakes have cooled 5 to 10 minutes, remove from the pans to a cooling rack.

As the layers cool, make the frosting by beating together the butter, sugar, peanut butter, and vanilla extract, adding just enough milk to make a creamy, spreadable frosting. Thinly spread the frosting on two layers of the cooled cake; pile the frosted layers together, and add the unfrosted layer on top. Use the remaining frosting to cover the outside of the whole cake.

MAKES 1 THREE-LAYER CAKE

Peanut Butter Pie

Although it sounds like child's food (and children do tend to like it), peanut butter pie is fundamental to the serious-dessert repertoire of the South. That's especially true in the peanut-rich state of Georgia, where you might also encounter peanut butter cake and peanut butter custard. This creamy, peanutty pie is on the Blue Willow Inn dessert table every day, and according to Louis Van Dyke, customers have been known to fight over what appears to be the last piece. Usually, it isn't. When one pie gets down to its last couple of pieces, the kitchen usually has another to take its place.

---

1   (8-ounce) package cream cheese
1   cup powdered sugar
1   cup crunchy peanut butter
1   (12-ounce) package refrigerated whipped topping
2   graham cracker pie shells

In a bowl mix the cream cheese, sugar, and peanut butter together. Fold in the topping, reserving enough to decorate the tops of the two pies. Pour the mixture into the pie shells, and chill several hours. Top each slice with a dab of topping.

MAKES 2 PIES

Pralines

Pralines are most often associated with New Orleans, where French-ancestored chefs originally pounded sugar and nuts into a fine paste that was supposed to be good for one's digestive tract. Sweet as they are, pralines are now beloved throughout the South.

1½	tablespoons light corn syrup
½	cup evaporated milk
3	tablespoons butter
½	cup brown sugar, firmly packed
1	cup sugar
⅛	teaspoon salt
½	cup pecan halves, toasted
½	cup pecan pieces, toasted
1	teaspoon vanilla

Combine the corn syrup, milk, butter, brown sugar, sugar, and salt in a buttered, heavy, 2-quart saucepan. Cook the mixture over medium heat, stirring frequently until blended and the temperature reaches 240°F on a candy thermometer. Add the pecans, and continue cooking until the temperature reaches 246°F. Remove the mixture from the heat, and let it cool for 2 minutes. Beat in the vanilla with a spoon until creamy. Immediately drop spoonfuls of the mixture onto wax paper making 2-inch circles. The candy should drop easily from the spoon. If the candy hardens before you have finished, add a few drops of milk, reheat, and stir until creamy. Store in a sealed container, separating layers with waxed paper.

MAKES 2 TO 2½ DOZEN

Pumpkin Pie

Although sweet potato pie is more common on local menus, pumpkin pies frequently appear on the dessert table in the Blue Willow buffet room. The Van Dykes say that whipped topping is optional. If serving the pie warm, a scoop of vanilla ice cream is a fine alternative embellishment.

1	(29-ounce) can 100% pure pumpkin
4	eggs
1½	cups granulated sugar
½	cup dark brown sugar
1	teaspoon salt
2	teaspoons cinnamon
2	cups milk
2	(9-inch) pie shells

Preheat the oven to 350°F. In a large bowl combine the pumpkin, eggs, sugars, salt, cinnamon, and milk, mixing well. Pour the mixture into the pie shell. Bake for 30 minutes. Serve warm or cold. If desired, top with whipped topping.

MAKES 16 SERVINGS

Pineapple Upside Down Cake

There isn't enough pineapple upside down cake in the world. It's a familiar dessert to most eaters, and yet it's almost never found in restaurants; and we don't know too many home cooks who bother to make it just the way it should be made, with a bright red cherry in the center of each pineapple ring. As a bastion of culinary tradition, the Blue Willow Inn keeps it in the regular dessert rotation; and whenever we see it, we smile like we are seeing a good old friend.

1	(18 ¼-ounce) box yellow cake mix
¼	cup butter
½	cup light brown sugar
1	cup pineapple juice
1	(20-ounce) can pineapple rings (drain and reserve juice)
	Maraschino cherries without stems

To make the batter, follow the directions on the cake mix box, except substitute pineapple juice for the water (or as much as you can). To make the glaze, combine the butter, brown sugar, and 1 cup pineapple juice in a saucepan, and bring to a boil. Remove from the heat. Preheat the oven to 350°F. Layer the bottom of a lightly greased, 10 x 10-inch baking pan with the pineapple rings, and place a cherry in the center of each ring. Pour the warm glaze over the pineapples. Pour the prepared cake mix evenly over the pineapple rings. Bake for 35 minutes, or until a sharp knife inserted in the center of the cake comes out clean. After removing the cake from the oven, cover the baking pan with a larger pan. Carefully turn the cake upside down, and gently remove it from the baking pan into the larger pan.

MAKES 8 TO 10 SERVINGS

Petra's "Just Right" Pound Cake

When having a bridge club luncheon, pound cake is almost always the preferred dessert. We like this one just about any time of day, especially for an afternoon snack and even at breakfast with a cup of coffee. It comes from the Van Dykes's late friend Petra Broberg. They speculate that one reason her cake was always so good is that after the batter was poured into the pan, she eliminated any air pockets by banging it hard on the kitchen counter. Whenever she served it, she would apologize, "It just isn't right." But, of course, it was always just right.

2	sticks butter
3	cups sugar
6	eggs
1	cup sour cream
½	teaspoon baking soda
3	cups all-purpose flour, sifted
1	teaspoon vanilla

Grease and flour a tube pan. Preheat the oven to 350°F. Cream the butter and sugar thoroughly in a mixer. Add the eggs gradually, one at a time, continuing to beat the butter. Allow at least 1 minute of beating between adding each egg. Add the sugar, and beat more. In a small bowl mix the sour cream and baking soda. Add this to the egg mixture a little at a time, alternating with the flour, beating all the time. Finally, add the vanilla. Pour the batter into the prepared tube pan. Tap the pan on the counter several times to eliminate any air pockets in the batter. Bake for 1 hour, or until light brown. Test the cake by inserting a toothpick in the center. When it comes out clean, the cake is done.

MAKES 1 LARGE POUND CAKE

Punch Bowl Cake

On Thanksgiving and Mother's Day, special-occasion dishes are featured at every station from the salad bar to the dessert table. One of those extra-extravagant desserts is Punch Bowl Cake, made from a recipe brought to the kitchen by Blue Willow Inn employee Keith Browning. It's one of those wonderful easy-does-it recipes that requires virtually no kitchen drudgery but turn out utterly baroque in their majesty.

1	*(18-¼-ounce) box yellow cake mix*
1	*(20-ounce) can crushed pineapple*
2	*(12-ounce) packages refrigerated whipped topping*
1	*(12-ounce) package shredded coconut, divided in half*
¼	*plus ¼ cup chopped pecans*
1	*(20-ounce) can cherry pie filling*

Bake the cake according to the directions on the box, creating two layers. Allow the cake to cool. Crumble one layer of the cake into the bottom of a punch bowl along with one-half of the coconut. Spread the crushed pineapple over the layer of coconut and cake. Use one container of the topping to top the pineapple. Top this layer with ¼ cup pecans. Crumble the second layer of cake over the pecans. Spread the remaining one-half coconut and the cherry pie filling atop the second layer of cake. Top with the second container of topping, and top that with the remaining ¼ cup pecans. Refrigerate for 6 to 8 hours to allow the flavors to mingle.

MAKES 1 (2-LAYER) CAKE

Rice Pudding

In coastal Georgia, where the Van Dykes grew up, rice is the fundamental starch. It is not uncommon to prepare large quantities so that you have not only enough to accompany your seafood gumbo, but also to have several cups left over to make a batch of this elementary and always excellent rice pudding. To transform it from comfort food into a luxury dessert, serve the warm pudding in a bowl topped with heavy cream and a few fresh berries.

4	cups cooked rice
1½	cups sugar
4	cups milk
1	cup raisins
½	teaspoon nutmeg
4	eggs, slightly beaten
	Dash of salt

Preheat oven to 350°F. In a large bowl combine the rice, sugar, milk, raisins, nutmeg, eggs, and salt. Mix well, and pour into a casserole. Bake for 1½ hours, or until the top is browned. Serve warm.

MAKES 8 SERVINGS

Red Velvet Cake

Yes, it really is vivid red! This old-fashioned bit of kitchen fun used to be popular throughout the country, but has remained so only in places where traditions die hard, i.e. the South. It has the flavor of a childhood birthday cake; and white cream cheese frosting is de rigueur.

Cake:

1½	cups sugar
1	cup shortening
2	large eggs
2	(2-ounce) bottles red food color
2	tablespoons cocoa
2¼	cups all-purpose flour
1	teaspoon salt
1	cup buttermilk
1	tablespoon vinegar
1	teaspoon soda

Frosting:

1	(1-pound) box confectioners' sugar
½	teaspoon vanilla
1	(8-ounce) package cream cheese, softened
½	cup chopped pecans
4	tablespoons margarine, softened

Preheat the oven to 350°F. To make the cake, in a bowl cream the sugar and shortening. Add the eggs one at a time. In a separate bowl make a paste with the food coloring and cocoa. Add the paste to the shortening mixture. In another bowl combine the flour and salt, and add to the mixture. In a cup mix the buttermilk, vinegar, and soda, and add to the mixture. Pour the mixture into three greased and floured, 8-inch layer pans. Bake for 25 to 30 minutes, or until done. Let the cake cool in the pan before removing.

To make frosting, in a bowl cream together the sugar, vanilla, cream cheese, pecans, and margarine until light and fluffy. If the frosting is too thin, add more confectioners' sugar.

MAKES ONE 3-LAYER CAKE

Strawberry Shortcake

Southerners are blessed with a long growing season, which means that ripe fruits are available for most of the year. When the strawberries are at their biggest and sweetest is the time to make this shortcake.

1	quart fresh strawberries, plump and juicy
1/3	cup sugar plus 1½ tablespoons
2½	cups all-purpose flour
½	tablespoon baking powder
½	teaspoon salt
½	teaspoon baking soda
½	cup butter, softened
1	(¼-ounce) package yeast
⅛	cup lukewarm water
½	cup buttermilk
⅔	cup (1 stick plus 3 tablespoons) butter, melted
	Refrigerated whipped topping

Slice the strawberries, place them in a container, and sprinkle them with the ⅓ cup sugar. Cover the strawberries, and refrigerate while baking the cake.

For the cake, in a bowl combine the 1½ tablespoons sugar, flour, baking powder, salt, and baking soda. Cut in the butter until the mixture resembles coarse meal. In a small dish dissolve the yeast in the warm water. Add the dissolved yeast to the dry ingredients. Add the buttermilk, and blend thoroughly. Preheat the oven to 450°F. Turn the dough onto a lightly floured board, and roll it out to a ¼-inch thickness. Cut the dough with a biscuit cutter. Dip the rounds in the melted butter. Place the rounds on a baking sheet (do not grease), and bake for 15 minutes. Top the cooled cakes with strawberries and their juice. Top the strawberries with a generous portion of whipped topping.

MAKES 12 TO 15 CAKES

Sugar Cookies

This is a basic recipe that can be colored and shaped to fit season, mood, or holiday.

Cookies:
- 1 cup melted butter
- 1½ cups sugar
- 1 egg
- 1 teaspoon vanilla
- ½ teaspoon almond extract
- 2½ cups all-purpose flour
- 1 teaspoon baking soda
- 1 teaspoon cream of tartar

Icing (optional):
- ⅓ cup butter, softened
- 3 cups confectioners' sugar
- 1½ teaspoons vanilla extract
- 2 tablespoons milk

In a large bowl thoroughly mix the butter, sugar, egg, vanilla, and almond extract. Blend in the flour, baking soda, and cream of tartar. Cover, and chill for 2 to 3 hours. Preheat the oven to 375°F. Remove the dough from the refrigerator. Roll out the dough on a lightly floured cutting board. Cut it into desired shapes, and cook on a sheet pan for 9 to 11 minutes, or until golden brown at the edges. Let cool before serving.

In a mixing bowl blend the butter and sugar. Stir in the vanilla. Add the milk to make a consistency to spread. Spread the icing over cooled cookies. Add food colorings and toppings to fit the season.

MAKES ABOUT 5 TO 6 DOZEN

Tea Cakes

This is the simplest kind of cake to serve with tea because these bite-sized dainties require no utensils. They do, however, demand plenty of napkins, lest powdered sugar fall all over ladies' laps.

1	cup sugar
½	pound (2 sticks) butter, softened
1	cup oil
2	large eggs
2	teaspoons vanilla
4½	cups all-purpose flour
1	teaspoon baking soda
1	teaspoon baking powder
1	teaspoon cream of tartar
1	cup confectioners' sugar
	Sifted confectioners' sugar for topping

Preheat the oven to 325°F. In a bowl cream the sugar, butter, oil, eggs, and vanilla. Add the flour, baking soda, baking powder, cream of tartar, and confectioners' sugar. Using a teaspoon, drop portions of the mixture onto a baking sheet. Bake for 15 minutes. Sprinkle with sifted powdered sugar while still warm.

MAKES ABOUT 5 DOZEN

Watermelon Cake

A sweet, summery, light as air, delicious, and easy way to please your guests.

Cake:

1	tablespoon all-purpose flour
1	(18 ¼-ounce) box white cake mix
1	(3-ounce) package mixed fruit-flavored gelatin
¾	cup vegetable oil
1	cup cut-up watermelon pieces
4	eggs

Preheat the oven to 325°F. In a large bowl sprinkle the flour over the cake mix. Add the gelatin, oil, and watermelon. Mix thoroughly with an electric mixer, adding the eggs one at a time. Divide the batter into 2 greased and floured 8-inch pans. Bake for about 30 minutes. Add the icing when the cake has cooled.

Icing:

1	stick margarine
1	(16-ounce) box confectioners' sugar
½	to 1 cup cut-up watermelon

Soften the margarine, and add the sugar. Blend in the watermelon gradually until a spreading consistency is reached. Red food coloring may be added for effect. Spread the icing generously over the cake.

This is really having your cake and being blessed to eat it, too.

MAKES ONE 2-LAYER CAKE

White Chocolate Macadamia Nut Cookies

When the Blue Willow Inn was struggling to survive, the Van Dykes's banker, Sandra Conner, often offered words of encouragement, telling them she had faith in their ability to make the restaurant work . . . and finally offering them this recipe for irresistible cookies. The Van Dykes suggest doubling the recipe, "as these go fast!"

½	cup butter
½	cup shortening
¾	cup packed brown sugar
½	cup sugar
1	large egg
1½	teaspoons vanilla
2	cups all-purpose flour
1	teaspoon baking soda
6	ounces white chocolate chips
7	ounces macadamia nuts

Preheat the oven to 350°F. In a bowl combine the butter, shortening, brown and white sugars, egg, vanilla, flour, baking soda, chips, and nuts, and mix well. Drop by the tablespoonful onto a lightly greased baking pan. Bake for 8 to 10 minutes.

MAKES 2 TO 4 DOZEN COOKIES

ACKNOWLEDGMENTS

First, we thank Billie and Louis Van Dyke for having created the Blue Willow Inn. Their devotion to a beautiful vision of southern food is an inspiration for those of us with a dream in any walk of life. We thank them also for their hospitality while we spent time in Social Circle and their indefatigable help and enthusiasm from the very beginning of this project.

We are also deeply indebted to the good people at Thomas Nelson who have given us the opportunity to commemorate one of our favorite restaurants in a favorite way: by making its story and its recipes into this book. In particular, we thank Publisher Larry Stone, who has shared some great meals with us at America's best tables, and whose belief in the concept of a Roadfood cookbook made it happen. We also thank Geoff Stone for his scrupulous editing, Bryan Curtis for his good ideas to spread the word, and Roger Waynick for being the bright spark that ignited this whole idea.

Thanks also to agent Doe Coover for her tireless work on our behalf, and to Jean Wagner and Marcia Fallon, Mary Ann Rudolph and Ned Schankman for making it possible for us to travel in confidence that all's well at home.

—Jane and Michael Stern

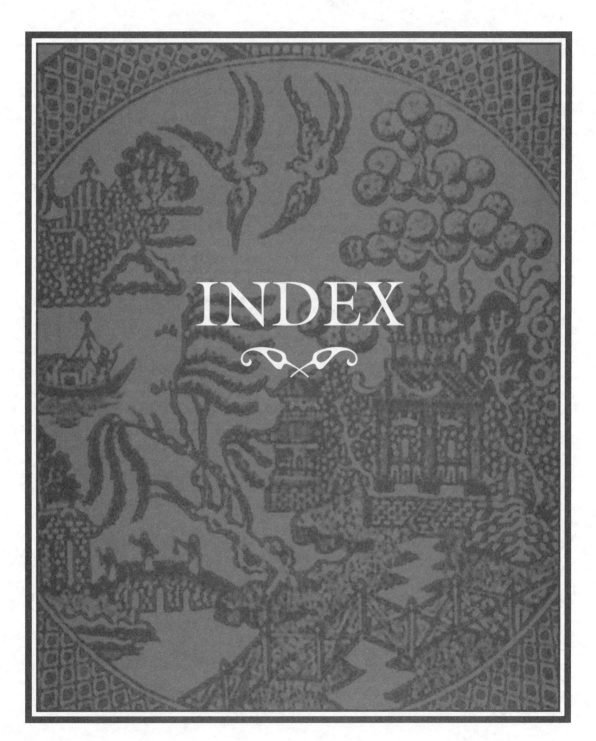

INDEX